CHRISTIAN HUMANISM

Christian Humanism

by

LOUIS BOUYER

Translated by

A. V. LITTLEDALE

THE NEWMAN PRESS

Westminster, Maryland, 1959

NIHIL OBSTAT: Carolus Davis, S.T.L.,
                    Censor deputatus
IMPRIMATUR: + Georgius L. Craven
                    Epūs Sebastopolis Vic. Gen.

Westmonasterii, die 18a Aug. 1958

Made and printed in Great Britain by Butler & Tanner Ltd.,
Frome and London.

© Copyright 1958, Geoffrey Chapman Ltd., London

CONTENTS

PREFACE

THIS book expresses a feeling of uneasiness, or, rather, of alarm. The early part of the present century was disfigured by the modernist crisis in the Church. A recurrence of that crisis may appear quite unthinkable, and yet, it would seem, there are those who are doing all in their power to bring it about. They are like the émigrés of old, returning from exile, having learnt nothing and forgotten nothing. To read certain books is to gain the impression that modernism has already re-emerged. Not that we are threatened with a fresh crisis, but with a fruitless resurgence of one we thought extinct.

This time, however, the cause does not lie in an intoxication with results of historical research or a particular philosophy of religion, both very questionable. It is to be found, rather, in the mental uncertainty prevalent in a turbulent age, joined to a kind of intellectual demagogy eager to baptise every fashion of thought on its first appearance.

In view of this, it is only natural that the enthusiasts for an imaginary past, the closed and petrified thinkers, the specialists in denunciation, should rejoice that their time has come. What a marvellous opportunity for them to create in the Church a climate of suspicion, to discourage any real activity of mind, to impugn any persons of vision!

The trouble is that the first modernist crisis widened

catastrophically the breach between the apostolate and the world it envisaged. A second would, perhaps, impair the Church's action to the extent of leaving her isolated from the world which would ignore her completely.

The purpose of this essay is to appeal to Catholics, the clergy in particular, not to repeat the mistake of identifying the truth with one extreme or other. Orthodoxy does not consist in refusing to accept facts or to think. To be modern does not imply a blind following of fashion. Nor does truth lie in holding mutually incompatible positions, but in seeing deeper than the verbalism of ready-made solutions of whatever kind.

I

GOD WITH US

RELIGION is natural to man, but equally naturally his religions tend to idolatry. What Voltaire said is only too true, that, if God made man to his own image, man makes God in his. There is probably no one, however apparently irreligious, who does not adore someone or something. But there are few, even among the most religious, who do not, to some extent, project themselves into their object of worship.

The religion of Israel, of the prophets, is, primarily, the most uncompromising rejection, the most outspoken of protests against this inward corruption, this original sin common to all religions in so far as they are human. 'I will not give my glory to another' are the words wherewith God himself, in the book of Isaias, denounces idolatry, and the recurring theme of the whole book. The first commandment of the decalogue, prescribing the worship of God, defines this duty by condemning what infringes it. 'Thou shalt not make to thyself a graven thing, nor the likeness of anything that is in heaven above, or in the earth beneath, nor of those things that are in the waters under the earth. Thou shalt not adore them nor serve them. I am the Lord thy God, jealous, visiting the iniquity of the fathers upon the children, unto the third and fourth generation of them that hate me; and showing mercy unto thousands of

9

them that love me, and keep my commandments'
(*Exod.* xx. 4–6).

The devout Israelite continually recalled the words of
Deuteronomy, 'Hear, O Israel, the Lord thy God is one
God. Thou shalt love the Lord thy God with thy whole
heart, and with thy whole soul, and with thy whole
strength' (vi. 5).

God, the true God, is the only God. He is in Heaven,
and man is on the earth, which means that he is beyond
our understanding. When David aspires to build for God
a house beside his own, this is what God said to him:
'Heaven is my throne, and the earth my footstool. What
is this house that you will build to me? And what is this
place of my rest? My hand made all these things' (Isa.,
lxvi. 1–2). In other words, God and his power are not to
be seized by man, enclosed in a place considered sacred,
domesticated, so to speak, by ritual observances which
would place them at man's disposition, or his pleasure
. . . 'I will give my glory to no other'.

Yet the God of Sinai, of Heaven, of the mountain man
may not venture to go near, the God who crushes those
who approach him with presumption, himself, on Sinai
too, draws near to man in his mercy, so that they exclaim:
'There is no other nation so great that hath gods so nigh
to them, as our God is present to all our petitions'
(*Deut.*, iv. 7).

This same God who dwells not in temples made with
hands, whom the heavens cannot contain, comes down,
veiled in a luminous cloud, to dwell with his people in a
tent, and to become the companion of their journeyings.
It is true, man must not mistake this condescension for a
surrender. When Solomon's temple had replaced the

tabernacle of Moses, and Israel, established in the Promised land, thought itself irrevocably possessed of the divine power, Jeremias proclaimed, from the very threshold of the sanctuary: 'Trust not in lying words, saying: The temple of the Lord, the temple of the Lord, it is the temple of the Lord . . . Go ye to my place in Silo, where my name dwelt from the beginning, and see what I did to it for the wickedness of my people Israel' (*Jer.*, vii. 4–12). Later, Ezechiel beheld the divine Presence abandoning the sanctuary polluted by idolatry, though the priests continued with their rites, void of all significance, without the slightest awareness of God's absence. But the Presence was not withdrawn completely. It remained now, invisible, unsuspected, with the exiles, the captives, in the land of Babylon. There they had no more ceremonial worship, no sanctuary, but the Presence itself became their sanctuary for the duration of their trial.

Subsequently, the rabbis proclaimed that where two or three Israelites devoutly met together to meditate on the Torah (the Law, the Word of God), the Shekinah, the Presence of God, was in the midst of them.

As is affirmed in the Bible, man cannot approach God and behold him without dying, but God himself approaches man to give him life. The towers of Babel man tries to build so as to reach to Heaven are destroyed by God when they are scarcely begun, and their builders dispersed. But God comes down to earth unheralded. He stretches his hand over Moses and hides him in a rock, when he passes before him. Then it is that Moses hears, not a word that strikes terror, but a promise which is more than a promise, a revelation of the very heart of God: 'O the Lord, the Lord God, merciful and gracious, patient and of much compassion and true, who keepest mercy unto thousands, who takest away iniquity and wickedness and sin, and no man of himself is innocent before thee . . . And Moses making haste bowed down prostrate and said: "If I have found grace in thy sight, O Lord, I beseech thee that thou wilt go with us, for it is a stiff-necked people, and take away our iniquities and sin, and possess us" ' (*Exod.*, xxxiv. 6–9).

Before that, Abraham, in obeying the call of God to leave his country, his family, his father's house (*Gen.*, xii.), for solitariness and exile, had encountered God. Nor had God shown himself in thunder and lightning, as the God of Heaven, Sovereign, the wholly Other, but in human guise, as a wanderer, a stranger on the earth, as a pilgrim passing by his tent at a time of day when all the rest were asleep, overcome by the heat, but Abraham alone was awake. Even before God had had time to ask for hospitality, Abraham had arisen and prostrated himself before him. He had seen three figures inseparable from one another, and adored the mystery of a single presence. In his simple joy and embarrassment, he brought in all the best things he had, the tenderest beast of the flock, bread quickly prepared in the manner of nomads, together with their greatest and lowliest possession, water to wash in and refresh the weariness of travelling in the open desert. The three who were one received it all in silence; but, when God sat at man's table and had apparently partaken of his food, he uttered this word never before heard, greater indeed than all the promises he went on to repeat: 'Shall I hide from Abraham what I shall do?' Abraham was now the friend of God, and what secrets could God withhold from him? Abraham understood this so well that he had no hesitation in putting a request, the boldest, we might almost say the most insolent, that could be made. What would be profanity, idolatry, in the case of a man claiming to equality with God, to possession of God, becomes faith and love when it is God who comes to man, makes himself man, gives himself to man. Not that God withdraws what he said: 'I will give my glory to no other', but that his Son himself says to him: 'Father, . . . the glory which thou hast given me, I have given to them, that they may be one as we also are one, I in them and thou in me, that they may be made perfect in one . . .' (*John*, xvii. 22–23). For the God of Heaven is not a far-off, remote God, but one who is close at hand. He who determines the number of the stars is also he who heals the contrite of heart, and binds their wounds.

Man does not know God; if he thinks he does, he deceives himself. He calls God the work of his hands, or else he adores as gods the greatest of God's works. In consequence, as soon as God begins to disclose himself, man is terrified. At Sinai, the Israelites run to Moses, and say: 'Speak thou to us and we will hear. Let not the Lord speak to us lest we die' (*Exod.* xx. 19). The epistle to the Hebrews says that 'Our God is a consuming fire', and 'It is a terrible thing to fall into the hands of the living God'.

The first thing God reveals to man about himself is that he is a hidden God. God first reveals himself as inaccessible. This does not mean that he is a God of darkness; he is light itself, but the light wherein he dwells is a light inaccessible.

Man does not know God, and he cannot know him until he has gone through the crucible which recasts him utterly. But God knows man. He knows of what we are made; he knows our weakness. He knows it, but does not despise it; rather, he has compassion on it, for he made us, and feels for us as a father. 'He hath not dealt with us according to our sins, nor rewarded us according to our iniquities. For according to the height of the heaven above the earth, he hath strengthened his mercy towards them that fear him. As far as the east is from the west, so hath he removed our iniquities from us. As a father hath compassion on his children, so hath the Lord compassion on them that fear him, for he knoweth our frame, he remembereth that we are dust' (*Ps.* cii. 10–14).

God knows us, then, in our weakness, and does not despise it. He has compassion on it, but he goes further. He knows in us what we cannot know, what does not yet exist in us, or hardly so. 'For if our heart reprehend us, God is greater than our heart, and knoweth all things' (1 *John,* iii. 20). He knows, not only that he made us, but that he made us to his image, and he cannot forget it however disfigured we be by sin, whether pride or sensuality; he still sees himself in us. Even when we no longer believe in him, he continues to believe in us; and when we despair of ourselves, he does not give up hope. Like the father of the prodigal son, he does not cease to regard as his son the one whom everyone else looks on as irretrievably outcast. With our first movement of repentance, we see him coming towards us, and we find ourselves again in his arms. We have no time even to stammer our halting explanations, for the feast of reconciliation is already prepared, a garment of light hides our wretchedness even from our own eyes, and the royal ring is put on our finger. God does more still, even more than the father of the prodigal. He is the shepherd who leaves the ninety-nine sheep who are safe, to go and seek out the one who is lost, and bring it back himself to the fold. He came into our world, put himself in our place, to 'seek and to save that which was lost'. And, when he has found it, he rejoices more, and invites his angels to rejoice more, for a single sinner who repents than for the ninety-nine just who have no need to repent. The prophets are at a loss to explain this love for man, so surpassing reason as to appear unreasonable. Osee can only liken it to a mysterious passion a good man suddenly feels, not for a woman who deserves it, but for the most degraded, the apparently most hardened, prostitute. He does not hesitate to ascribe to God a quite human sensibility, what he calls bowels of mercy. Jeremias, later, attributes the same pity to God, a pity which is also a real piety, which Osee had said that God desired to see, above all other things, in the heart of man. Ezechiel, going still further than Osee, compares God's love for man, not simply with love one might have for a degraded woman, but with a wholly incomprehensible affection that would lead to choosing for adoption an abortive child abandoned at birth by its own parents. What, then, is the meaning of the limitless love of the God of all majesty and holiness for a being utterly beneath him, and degraded too? It is, once again, that God sees in it what it is quite incapable of seeing itself—no illusion, however, or unrealisable dream, but a reality hidden, for the present, from everyone. This reality is expressed by Ezechiel in most unexpected fashion. When he sees the divine Presence, the Presence that has, so to speak, been thrust out of the sanctuary by the idolatry of its pretended worshippers, he makes use of an abundance of images to convey the sense of its incomparable splendour. But what, in this dazzling glory, does he see, above the four living creatures who are, as it were, the Angels of the cosmos, above even the firmament? Someone seated, someone who has, he says, the appearance of a human form, though this form is all unendurable brightness, consuming fire.

It is not only love for men, a love incomprehensible, that the prophets attribute to the great and terrible God, the jealous God, but also, we hardly dare to say, humanity. Only too readily do we, in our rational, not to say rationalistic, way of thinking, cast aside what we call the anthropomorphism of the Bible. Yet this way of speaking of God as a man, so often recurring, is no less essential to its message than the representations of God as a heavenly, invisible Being, who inhabits light inaccessible. The same God of Heaven who comes down to the earth like lightning, striking terror and death into whoever comes near him without reverence, the God whom no one can see without dying, is described as walking in the garden of Eden and conversing familiarly with Adam and Eve. He appeared to Abraham as the flame which passed, in the middle of the night, between the divided victims, but he was also his guest and sat at table with him. And to Moses, at the very time of the fiery manifestation on Sinai, he was said to appear as a friend with whom one speaks face to face.

Are we, then, back again, after much meandering, at the position which aroused Voltaire's sarcasm, simply imagining God like ourselves, on the ground that he made us to his image? Far from it; what we have done is to recognise the whole mystery of the relations of God with man. It is a mystery, because it is not a simple truth; a mystery, because at first sight a paradox. As for falling into idolatry, we are guilty of that only if we get rid of the paradox by simply ignoring one side of it, instead of going further and penetrating the luminous night of the mystery in which faith perceives, united, elements to all appearances incompatible.

Man cannot attain to God; if he thinks he can, he deceives himself, taking for God what is only an idol of his own imaging. If he did come to see God, the vision would kill him. But God can come to man, and wills to; and his coming means life to us, the true life, and, for that reason, life eternal.

God is wholly other than man, but in his eyes man is another himself. We talk of loving God, as if that were perfectly natural and easy, but, in fact, we are quite incapable of it. But God loves us, and his love knows no bounds. He made us to his image, to know and love him as he knows and loves us. He has made us to his image, and that itself is the greatest of his gifts. We, for our part, have come to form an entirely wrong idea of this, seeing it as something belonging to us by right, to be used as we please. We desire to own ourselves as our own property, thinking it no robbery to be equal with God; and so we forfeit everything. We are fallen, as the Fathers say, into the land of dissemblance. From being friends of God we are become his enemies. We know him no longer, and, were we to know him again as he is, it would be our death.

He, however, has not changed, has not stopped knowing and loving us as he knows and loves us in his eternity.

B

He knows fully that what he loves in us is but nothingness, but a nothingness restored, animated by his love
alone. He loves us, then, in our fallen state, our alienation. We cannot return to him again, but he rejoins us.
We could not possibly attain to his heavenly sanctuary,
but he makes himself our sanctuary in our place of exile.
Our attempts to confine him in temples built by the
hand of man are as futile, even more so, as our endeavour
to build ourselves here an abiding city. But once he has
made us aware that we are always pilgrims and travellers
in search of the city to come, he comes down to live in
his tent along with us. Then we can really tend to him
as our end, to the truth and life we so much need; but
only because he has made himself our way, and in so far
as we acknowledge this.

The travellers to Emmaus, unaware that they were
pilgrims, grieved that the divine Presence, seemingly
established on earth, had suddenly withdrawn. No doubt,
they had failed to understand what they had been told,
'It is expedient for you that I go.' But, on reaching their
destination, they broke bread together, in company with
him who seemed at first to be simply another traveller.
Then they knew him, in the breaking of bread. They
knew him, but only when they saw him no more. Such
is the presence of God with us, in Christ, in the Eucharist.
It is, as it were, the final outcome of God's age-long
endeavour to rediscover us in our remoteness, to restore
in us the lost likeness, to reunite us in the love we had
scorned. The Word of God, that Word in whom, for our
sakes as for his own, he expresses himself eternally, his
only Son, in whom he willed to adopt us all, began to
draw near to us from the first beginnings of human

history. As St Irenaeus says, he familiarised himself, little
by little, with the sons of men. He made himself the
guide and shepherd of Israel. He was with them in the
cloud, invisible; he protected them and led them in the
desert. Between the cherubims, in the empty space above
the propitiatory, it was he who spoke to them. Moses and
Aaron could both hear and see him; only, when these
elect of God returned to the people, they had to veil
their faces on account of the splendour of the Presence
reflected there. Now the Presence has itself set up his
tent on earth, in the sacred body of Christ, born of the
Spirit above and of the Virgin Mary. The Word has
become flesh, and his tabernacle is the flesh that gives
life to the world, the bread of life come down from
heaven. With Moses, our fathers ate manna in the desert,
and are dead; but here is the true, living bread come
down from heaven, and he who eats it shall not die. All
of us are called, with open face, to reflect as in a mirror
the glory of the Lord, contemplating by faith the risen
Christ, so as to be transformed into the same image,
from glory to glory, as by the Spirit of the Lord (2 *Cor.,*
iii. 17).

We must make no mistake about what this means.
There is no question of relapsing into idolatry. God is
not to be taken to will to consecrate the world as our
sins have made it, but his will is to recall it to its original
state. God did not will to become man so that man
might henceforth think he has the right to deify himself.
He became man in order to renew in man the image of
God. God took upon himself the full burden of sinful
humanity, death included, to raise up a race of children
of God. The resurrection, however, is not just the making

immortal of man as he now is, but is his entire remaking. It involves of necessity the death of the old man, born of the earth, that there may be reborn the new man, born from above, born of heaven. 'God so loved the world that he gave his only-begotten Son, that whosoever believes in him may not perish, but may have life everlasting' (*John*, iii. 16). This eternal life is 'to know thee, the one true God, and Jesus Christ whom thou hast sent' (*John*, xvii. 3).

Eating the bread of life, the bread of heaven, is to build up the interior man, the new man, the heavenly man, who is renewed precisely in the degree in which the earthly man, the old man, no more now than a mere husk, dies once and for all to rise no more. No doubt, the whole of man, the whole of creation, is to be saved, the body as well as the soul, the world in its entirety with man. But 'flesh and blood cannot possess the kingdom of God'. As the apostle himself tells us, the seed sown on earth must first die, for the grain to be born; and that which is sown is not the same as what will be reaped.

Christ, henceforth, is our life, 'but our life is hidden with Christ in God. When Christ our life shall appear, then only shall we also appear'. 'It hath not yet appeared what we shall be, but we know that when he shall appear we shall be like to him, because we shall see him as he is.'

Christ, the eucharistic Christ, is the final incarnation of the love of God for man. He is the final outcome of the will of God to be with us, to associate himself with us on earth, since we had become incapable of rejoining him above, in his only real sanctuary, the heavenly sanctuary, where he dwells in light inaccessible.

But Christ did not join himself to us to immobilise us in ourselves. On the contrary, he made himself a stranger and pilgrim to make us aware that that is what we are, that we have not, and cannot have here, an abiding city, but we look for one to come, the heavenly city whose foundations are eternal. He made himself our precursor with the Father, and, whenever the Eucharist is enacted, we adore him as having entered first into the heavenly sanctuary, as there exhibiting, on the propitiatory of his own body, the blood of reconciliation, as ever living in the presence of God, in order to draw us unfailingly, by his intercession, to the heavenly place, to the place he has gone to prepare for us, before returning to take us with him, that where he is we also may be, that we may be consummated in one, he in us and we in him, as he is in the Father and the Father in him.

II

THE CREATION AND THE CROSS

CHRISTIANITY, like Judaism, is in the first place an act of faith in the creation, for it asserts that all that exists comes from God, and that each thing, by the very fact of its existence, pays homage to the goodness, the wisdom and the power of the Creator. In this respect, the optimism of both religions is as thorough and comprehensive as possible. It is sometimes alleged that Christianity has impoverished the world on the pretext of leading man to holiness, and that the virtues it instils involve a mutilation of his being. We may say, without hesitation, that a Christianity guilty of this would be, by that very fact, untrue to its nature, radically falsified. We should not be misled by some expressions to be found in Scripture and Tradition. It is true that St Paul fulminates against the 'flesh', and St John is, if anything, even more uncompromising about the 'world'. The former tells us that 'they that are Christ's have crucified the flesh, with its vices and concupiscences' (*Gal.*, v. 24), and he explains this by the fact that 'flesh and blood cannot possess the Kingdom of God' (1 *Cor.*, xv. 50). St. John, for his part, declares unequivocally: 'Love not the world, nor the things which are in the world, . . . the whole world is seated in wickedness' (1 *John,* ii. 15 and v. 19). But the question is, what exactly do they mean? To see in these expressions a pessimism about the life of the body, or in regard to the universe to which it is bound, is to admit a basic contradiction.

When St Paul speaks of the 'flesh', he does not mean the body, in contrast with the soul. He uses the word to signify the whole man, spirit as well as body, as he is as a result of abandoning God, who is the source of all life, physical and spiritual. Crucifying the flesh, with its vices and concupiscences, is therefore, as he says elsewhere, to mortify our members which are upon the earth, which he goes on to explain as 'fornication, uncleanness, lust, evil concupiscence and covetousness, which is the service of idols' (*Col.*, iii. 5). Consequently, the 'flesh and blood' which cannot possess the kingdom of God is simply sinful man, left to himself, unable to attain sanctity and the real life by the use of his vitiated powers. Christ, on the other hand, by renewing us wholly in his Spirit, 'shall quicken also (our) mortal bodies' (*Rom.*, viii. 11). He will bring about 'the redemption of our body' (viii. 23) to such effect that we may be able to make of our bodies 'a living sacrifice, holy, pleasing unto God', which is, he says, our reasonable service (xii. 1). Earlier in the same epistle, the apostle makes quite clear what this offering of our bodies implies. 'Let not sin therefore reign in your mortal bodies, so as to obey the lusts thereof. Neither yield your members as instruments of iniquity unto sin; but present yourselves to God as those that are alive from the dead, and your members as instruments of justice unto God' (vi. 12–13). In fact, this living sacrifice of our bodies is of such a positive nature that St Paul goes so far as to call them temples of God. 'Know you not that your members are the temple of the Holy Ghost who is in you?' he says to the Corinthians, and he gives as his reason that their bodies are the members of Christ (1 *Cor.*, vi. 19 and 15). Nor can he conceive an eternal life which would be confined to the soul. The object of the whole magnificent Chapter XV of the first epistle to the Corinthians is to establish that the eternal life awaiting the Christian is the life of risen man in his entirety, body as well as soul, and to describe the glory destined for the body as well as the soul.

There is even less ground for us to be misled or dismayed by St John's statement that 'the whole world is seated in wickedness', and his injunction not to love the world or the things that are in it. Just as, with St Paul, the word 'flesh' is not just a synonym for 'body', the 'world', in St John's language, does not mean the physical universe as such, but in its condition as resulting from sin and from the rebellion of creatures against their Creator, which has brought them into captivity to Satan, the enemy of God. The world in itself, so far from falling under the condemnation of St John, is the object of that wonderful sentence of Christ preserved for us by the evangelist, who enshrines it at the heart of his narrative: 'God so loved the world that he gave his only-begotten Son, that whosoever believeth in him may not perish, but may have everlasting life' (iii. 16). Consequently, to refuse to love the world as it is, dominated by the forces of evil, is an indispensable condition for loving it truly, loving it as God loves it, God its Creator, to whom it is so dear that he did not hesitate to give, for its salvation, his only Son.

The Gospel, then, by no means goes back on the early part of Genesis, so full of wonder and confidence, but, in fact, brings out its final consequences. The very prologue repeats that it was by his Word that God made all things, and nothing was made but by this Word of love and holiness. All that exists is therefore holy, is a living homage to the Love of God, bodies as well as souls, the physical universe along with the world of spirits. So far is the Word of God from inciting us to despise anything, that it teaches us to hold all in admiration, to see in all things, in every being, so to speak a substantial echo of the divine word; we are enjoined to give thanks to God for every creature, for all that exists. Hence we have the exultant canticle at the end of the psalter, in which all creatures, from angels to men, from the stars to the elements, are called on to join in the homage of the faithful, so that the whole world, without distinction of matter and spirit, may become one harmonious choir, a single harp vibrating in accord under the breath of the Spirit of God.

Christianity is not guilty of casting a gloom over a world hitherto, under paganism, all light and joyful. On the contrary, it is when we compare the gospel with Greek and Latin paganism that we see the extent to which the Christian faith brought freedom to man. Paganism, as it drew to its end, may have known, as all civilisations in decline, outbursts of frenzied sense-indulgence, but it was singularly lacking in joy and peace. Its very sensuality had always despair in the background; the appetite for pleasure was invariably accompanied, and equally intensely, by an obsession with the transience of all things. To the pagans of old, evil, both in the world and in man, was not just accidental and surmountable, a prison they might hope to escape, but was bound up with the nature of things. The world as it is, man as we know him, had no possibility of emancipation from it. The physical world was simply the result of a degradation, a corruption of the divine nature, which had come to be embedded in matter, itself intrinsically evil. The restoration and reintegration of the world was quite inconceivable apart from the dissolution of existing reality. Man could not be saved, or rather his soul could not, except by flight from the world. His body was nothing more than the grave of his soul. No doubt it is quite an easy matter to indulge all the appetites of the body without restraint, but the body must still return to the slime of which it always forms part. As for the soul, it only begins to live when it abandons the body, without remorse, to its inevitable decay. If any kind of immortality can be had, it is only possible to a discarnate being, one that has abandoned and forgotten the world, viewing it as a prison incapable of being otherwise. If the soul has any commerce with the gods, it can only be on condition of foregoing all worldly interests and joys.

How different is the scriptural view of man and his destiny! Not only does the Bible proclaim that everything in this world was made by God, made wholly good, not only does the Gospel hold out to man the salvation of the body as well as of the soul, consecrating both body and soul to the glory of God, but its constant theme is that man is to bring about the plan of God and is his partner in the great work of creation. God blesses man's activity, primarily material, in the world, and his fecundity, even more, he enjoins it on man as his special task, the work assigned him, for which he was made, by which he is to realise the image of God in him which is

God's ideal for him. When God had seen that all the material creation was good, wholly good, he completed it by the creation of man. 'Then God said: Let us make man to our own image and likeness, and let him have dominion over the fishes of the sea, and the fowls of the air and the beasts and the whole earth, and every creeping creature that moveth upon the earth. And God created man to his own image, to the image of God he created him, male and female he created them. And God blessed them, saying: Increase and multiply and fill the earth, and subdue it, and rule over the fishes of the sea, and the fowls of the air, and all living creatures that move upon the earth' (*Gen.* i. 26–28). Again, in the second account: 'The Lord God took man, and put him into the paradise of pleasure, to dress it and to keep it' (ii. 15).

In view of this the Israelites held the supreme blessing to be a creative life, in which man, working with God, should make his field bear a profusion of corn, wine and oil, and his marriage be crowned with an abundance of healthy children.

While all this is true, and is not to be minimised or overlooked, it is also true that Christianity means the Cross. St Paul said to the Corinthians: 'I judged not myself to know anything among you but Jesus Christ, and him crucified' (1 *Cor.*, ii. 2). He was fully aware how unacceptable this was at first sight, that to the Greeks it was foolishness, to the Jews a scandal; but he considered that this foolishness of God was far wiser than all the wisdom of men, that it was the only wisdom worthy of the name. In his eyes, the importance of the Cross, of Christ's cross in the first place, lay in that it was the mystery, that is the fundamental secret, of the

Wisdom of God for the salvation of the world. In spite of appearances everything in the Bible from the very beginning led up to this alone. This Cross of Christ, on which the whole light of revelation is centred, is, too, the only possible key to the meaning of human history, whether profane—or appears to be so—or sacred. The cross of Christ, and it alone, is capable of unravelling the experience of mankind, both of each individual and of the whole human race. And the cross of Christ, let us make no mistake about it, involves our own. Christ died on the cross to save us, but that does not mean he died to save us from the necessity of dying. He died, rather, to give us courage to die as well, to help us to do so, to enable us to die in very deed. 'If we suffer with him,' says St Paul, 'we shall be also glorified with him' (*Rom.*, viii. 17). 'If we be dead with him, we shall live with him. If we suffer, we shall also reign with him' (2 *Tim.*, ii. 12). Baptism, as he interprets it, engrafts us in Christ's death, so that we may share, as well, in his resurrection.

Nor is this simply a piece of abstract mysticism; doubtless these are realities of a mystical kind, but they make real demands upon us which have to be translated into every detail of our lives. Once we have found Christ, or rather, when he has found us, all the rest, in St Paul's vigorous language, is but offscouring, and death itself is gain (*Phil.*, i. 21). Ultimately his supreme desire is 'to be dissolved, and to be with Christ' (i. 23).

The Christian, then, must willingly accept all sorts of trials, bodily as well as spiritual. Even more, he should go forward to meet them and deliberately undergo the discipline of asceticism. 'I chastise my body,' says St Paul, 'and bring it into subjection, lest perhaps, when I have preached to others, I myself should become a castaway' (1 *Cor.*, ix. 27). The whole of Christian life amounts to 'always bearing about in our body the mortification of Jesus' (2 *Cor.*, iv. 10).

St John himself, with all his mystical teaching on light and life, echoes St Paul, when he makes known to us the words of Christ, 'Unless the grain of wheat falling into the ground die, itself remaineth alone, but, if it die, it bringeth forth much fruit' (xii. 24–25). And he uses the expression 'lifted up' to signify both the raising up on the cross, and the glorious ascent to Heaven (xii. 32).

We are not entitled to tone down these passages by viewing them as a later systematisation of a single aspect of the life of Christ on the part of his followers from whose minds the Passion had tended to erase the memory of all that had preceded it, or who, at any rate, had come to consider it the salient feature in his life. For Christ's sayings on all sorts of occasions, as recorded by the synoptics, even when they contain no allusion at all to the Cross, are to the same purpose.

From the time he began to teach, Christ's purpose was not to proclaim, as the prophets had done, that the rich were accursed—the *evil* rich, as some would tell us—but that the poor were blessed, likewise those who mourned, and those who suffered persecution. He went even further and said: 'Everyone of you that doth not renounce all that he possesseth cannot be my disciple' (*Luke*, xiv. 33); and not only his possessions: 'If any man come to me, and hate not his father and mother and wife and children and brethren and sisters, yea and his own life also, he cannot be my disciple' (xiv. 26). After this, the explicit declaration: 'Whosoever doth not carry his cross and come after me cannot be my disciple' (27) adds nothing further, but follows of necessity. It may be urged that these passages come from St Luke, who had an obvious personal predilection for voluntary poverty in its strictest and most material sense. But here is something St Luke never ventured to report, his sensitivity recoiling before the uncompromising nature of the words: 'There are eunuchs who have made themselves eunuchs for the kingdom of heaven. He that can take it let him take it' (*Matt.*, xix. 12).

How is all this to be reconciled with the vision of the devout Israelite, with his children like olive-branches around his table, and his wife covering him with her shadow like a vine whose branches cling to a wall old but still firm? What is there in common between the adorer, himself crucified, of a God made man solely to die on a cross—'The Son of man is come not to minister unto, but to minister, and to give his life in redemption' (*Matt.*, xx. 28)— what has the Christian in common with the figure we have just seen who rejoices in admiration of the created world, and is himself destined to complete the great work of creation in the joy and satisfaction of fecundity?

We have here a problem that has exercised minds in every age, but has never been easy of solution. There has always been the temptation to surmount the paradox by ignoring one side. Today, however, perhaps more than previously, the temptation is particularly grave, and the problem urgent.

Man is clearly in a fair way to achieve final mastery over the forces of nature, subjected, as they are, to investigation by means hitherto undreamt of, and harnessed with a skill seemingly superhuman. Not only the scientist and the technologist, but the ordinary man, whose reading is virtually confined to the sports news, feels the intoxication of recent discoveries. Nothing seems impossible, there are no limits to what may be hoped for. With excellent reason it might be thought that man is on the very verge of putting the final touch to creation by stamping it with his own humanity, and, at the same time, attaining for himself a real super-humanity, making of himself a kind of demiurge, creator of his own destiny and that of the universe as well.

It is difficult for a Christian to view these hopes with detachment. He is aware of all that the scriptural doctrine of creation contains to support, enlighten and to direct to a noble purpose these intimations of modern man, who is, after all, his contemporary, whose concerns are his. It is tempting to say that these new powers over the world of nature placed at our disposal by modern civilisation are like a recovery of the preternatural gifts we lost, according to classical theology, as a result of the Fall.

But, if this is so, where does the Gospel of the cross come in? This question raises doubts and is certainly an awkward one. Many different answers are suggested. Some have recourse to the idea that there are many different vocations, quite distinct from one another. Now as always, there are in the Church those called to be ascetics, men and women who practise mortification, live in voluntary continence; they are a living witness to the Cross. This is reasonable and quite desirable, indeed, perhaps, necessary. But, they go on to say, it is no less necessary, now more than ever before, to have vocations of a creative kind, men and women dedicated to the work, equally excellent, of continuing and fulfilling the creation. Nor can it be said that these practise a Christianity void of asceticism. The case is, rather, that theirs is a positive asceticism, of a kind not yet sufficiently worked out in comparison with the negative practices of traditional monasticism. Religious, and priests too, if they really understood the times they live in, and the significance of this vocation and the enhanced position of the laity, would gain a renewed insight into their own calling. They would abandon the last relics of a neo-platonic asceticism which has, we are told, been only too successful in distorting the true conception of Christian asceticism. They would see what charity really is, that it is, as the apostle says, active, not just passive. What they themselves forego, they would gladly place at the disposal of the activities of others. If they renounced family life, or human occupations of a directly creative kind, it would be purely to assist, inspire and support the positive works of others. The mystical body would come to develop through the co-ordination of its members, whose various activities would be mutually complementary, and the general result would be not in any sense destructive, but a progressive and unimpeded advance of the work of creation.

Obviously, this suggested division of labour falls in well with the ideas of today, and such a fresh conception of the mystical body is apt to resolve all problems. But is it a real solution? Up to now, the Church has always upheld the principle that the state of virginity consecrated to Christ is higher than the married state, notwithstanding the excellences of the latter proclaimed by St Paul along with those of virginity. It has always held, as a consequence, that progress in the spiritual life may legitimately lead from one vocation, certainly of positive merit, to one more noble still; so that in the state of widowhood, and even in a married life, provided the vocation was well-tested, one might advance from the state of Christian marriage to the solitary life, for a greater and more direct fulfilment of the demands of charity.

Nowadays, an opposite view seems to be entertained. If the monastic, religious, priestly vocation is looked on as exceptional, and its only justification held to be that it is subsidiary to that of the layman, creative and pro-creative, which alone directly fulfils the final end of creation—what will happen? This is not difficult to foresee; in fact, foresight is superfluous, we have only to look, and see what is going on around us. How many priests and religious will not be tempted to believe that they will attain a fuller spiritual and human develop-ment, that they will advance from a merely preparatory vocation to their definitive one, if they exchange the altar for the workshop, the library or the laboratory, and, in fact, celibacy for marriage, or at least for 'sexual development', as modern jargon has it?

Nor could they be reproached on the above prin-ciples; for, if these are correct, they have simply followed them to their conclusions, and they cannot be blamed for being logical. It may be, however, that this very logic should lead us to look more closely into principles some-what hastily accepted.

There is another solution to the problem, and this,

c

certainly, takes account of the first objection encountered on examining the new theory of the mystical body
on which the former solution was grounded.

It is perfectly true that, in the mystical body, there is
a diversity, an extreme diversity, of callings; but that
must not mislead us into thinking that there is no one
law of life for all. The same body could not possibly
comprise members whose development followed principles diametrically opposed, or, to put it more precisely, members destined to self-development along with
others dedicated solely to renunciation. No doubt, the
early part of this century saw the birth and spread
within the Church of certain allegedly mystical theories
of compensation and substitution, according to which
the suffering, apparently inexplicable, of some members
of the mystical body was considered necessary to the
felicitous development of others. The Carmelite in her
life of mortification would, thus, act as a lightning-
conductor for the comfortable Christian with his after-
dinner pipe; the trappist who, we are told, spends his
whole life in suffering and so hastens to an early grave,
would thereby assure, by the appropriate adjustment of
a supernatural balance-sheet, the vigour of countless
Christian families and the prosperity of their under-
takings. Unfortunately, this marvellous law of compensation, in spite of being commended by Léon Bloy, has
been already contradicted by St Paul in explicit terms.
What he said is not: 'When one member suffers, all the
others rejoice', nor: 'When one member rejoices, all the
rest suffer', but exactly the opposite: 'When one member suffers, all suffer . . . when one rejoices, all rejoice'.

There is another way, recently proposed, of harmonising faith in the Creator and faith in the Crucified, and it is much more deserving of consideration. It admits that the creation has to explain the Cross, and not the other way round. But, we are told, the creation is something far more involved than Christian thinkers believed before the discoveries of modern science. We are, in fact, invited, in round terms, to dissociate the idea of creation from the neolithic notion of the divine fatherhood. Creation is, of its essence, progressive, evolutionary, and that is precisely why there is no opposition between it and the Cross. The Cross, or rather what it symbolizes for us, is anterior to creation, or, better, to creative evolution. For the latter, being a spiral movement, involves a continual transcending, and so a continual detachment from what it has already attained, and this is not thereby simply lost, but lost in order to be recovered anew, that is on a higher plane, and transfigured. In short, it is a question of Goethe's 'dying and becoming'. It follows that what we know as the Cross is inherent in, not opposed to, what we call creation. The Cross, or, more exactly, the necessary passivities of diminution and growth, corresponds to the forces of inertia to be overcome by the evolutionary drive: and it is precisely in the victory of the latter that it is ennobled and vindicated. These forces, then, we have no need to deplore; all we have to do is to understand them aright, and then to accept them in positive fashion. Obviously, the passivities of growth, the price to be paid for a progress directly, or almost directly, registered, raise no difficulty; but it is different with those of diminution, those leading, not to the development, but to the break up of

the being subject to them. But faith, rightly understood, allies itself simply with the positive vision which
endows the passivities of growth with a beneficent meaning. It teaches, that the end of evolution is not to be
grasped on the plane of the individual. Now that it is
so evident that all men are bound up with one another,
we cannot divorce our individual achievements from
those of the entire race. The sphere of the mind itself,
now that it has become clearly distinct from the bio-
sphere, is bound to polarise itself, in its totality, round
the point omega, which is the scientific term for what
the unenlightened Christian calls God. From this comprehensive standpoint, all the setbacks encountered by
the individual are seen to be caught up in the advance
of the whole. The fact is that there are no passivities
of diminution except on the level of the isolated individual; and if the latter, as he should, sees himself in
relation to the whole, which is his sole reason for existence—and this he does by gladly accepting what, in
any case, leaves him no alternative—his own passivities
of diminution are absorbed into the resultant growth
of the whole. Thus, even the worst disasters will be
finally resolved into the ultimate well-being of the
whole, when the evolutionary curve will have reached
its apex. All that remains for the individual to do is to
recognise the significance of the historical process, and
to submit to it, whatever the cost, without reserve.

It would be idle to deny the seduction this view exer-
cises on many minds today. Father Teilhard de Chardin,
by his way of clothing Christian spirituality in words
borrowed from modern science, seems to them a modern
Origen, or even a St Thomas.

Doubtless his theory has the great advantage over the former of setting forth a uniform law of the formation of the mystical body. The only drawback is that this uniformity would seem to make it impossible, when the time arrives, to distinguish the mystical body from any concentration camp.

Where it proves most unsatisfactory is that there are two things for which it finds no place, two discontinuities in a movement claiming to be uniform, too uniform, perhaps—the discontinuity of sin, by which we passed from the universe of creation to that of the Cross; and the discontinuity of the resurrection, which alone makes it possible for us to return, though by way of the Cross, to the first plan of creation, and to attain its ultimate fulfilment.

To grasp what this means, we shall have to go rather more deeply into the mystery of how our complete dependence on our Creator is bound up, though seemingly inconsistent, with our inalienable freedom. This will be the subject of the following chapter.

III
DEPENDENCE AND FREEDOM

THE main objection of modern man against religion,
and the Church in particular, is that it curtails his freedom. In the United States, for example, whose whole
legal system is grounded on a complete confidence in
man's creative possibilities, there are periodical sounds
of warning. The danger is seen that Catholics, making
as much use as others of these possibilities, may turn
them against liberty itself; that, should they become
a majority, and attain to power with the freedom to
organise the life of individuals as they please, the free
expression of opinion would be immediately threatened.
If we say that such fears are chimerical, that they mistake present-day Catholicism with that of a past age,
and, more precisely, with ideas that Catholics then
shared with the rest of the world, we are confronted
with the condemnations, rarely alluded to, of the
famous syllabus of Pius IX.

We see, too, in opposition both to Pius IX and to
the modern transatlantic controversialists, Catholics, in
France and elsewhere, who contend that what distin-
guishes living from dead Catholicism is the full acceptance, or the rejection—disguised it may be—of the
ideas of 1789. To speak more plainly, the acceptance,
without reserve or even discussion, of the principles of
freedom that are at the base of the modern democracies

is a necessary preliminary to any effective action, or, as the saying is, to any presence of the Church in the modern world.

What should be our attitude to these various statements and to these divergences of view which, manifestly, imply others even deeper?

When we consider the general attitude, not so much of the Church, but of Catholics, since 1789, we are struck by the twofold current present within the Church. There are those who, since they claim to be traditionalists, enjoy, for that reason, a certain benevolent regard on the part of authority. Nevertheless, it is very significant that the latter never comes down wholly on their side, and that the time invariably arrives when it warns them in a fatherly fashion, then openly censures them, and nearly always, sooner or later, condemns them. Those of whom we speak see the cause of the Church as one with that of authority, of all authority; they take a jaundiced view of freedom in any sphere whatever, still more when raised to an absolute value. At times, they draw a distinction, not without plausibility, between 'liberty' and 'the liberties'; they maintain, with ingenuity, that indeterminate liberty is a myth, and that it can only harm all the various kinds of concrete, well-defined, liberties. But they have to admit that this kind of distinction is looked on by the majority of the party with indifference, or else distrust; and even those who put it forward, once they believe, optimistically, that they are on the threshold of power, are liable to push their own distinctions into the background.

On the other hand, those whose general outlook is a

liberal one are not looked on by authority with any particular favour. In those activities of theirs which are admitted to be generous ones, even, and especially, when they are held to be ill-conceived, they come up against severe opposition, which, sooner or later, overwhelms them so suddenly and vehemently that they are crushed for a time. But it is very noticeable that authority takes the utmost pains not to stifle them completely. The traditionalists rejoice, but not for long; and, when they are on the point of giving the final blow to the prostrate enemy, they are frequently surprised to find that they have themselves become the target of attack, and are obliged to look on hopelessly and indignantly while authority itself restores the blasphemers they had hoped to remove.

There are, then, those who say that 'all power corrupts, and absolute power corrupts absolutely', and it is hardly surprising that authority looks on them unfavourably. On the other side are those who set authority on a pedestal; yet we observe that, when authority fails to act as they would wish, they have no hesitation in criticising it with a quite unexpected freedom. A very eminent ecclesiastic likens their attitude to that of the Papuan who prostrates himself before his idol, yet beats it if it does not give him at once all he asks. At the same time, how often do we not see liberals who, once they attain power, use it in the most despotic fashion? Their success is, of course, by very definition, the triumph of liberty, and they naturally exploit it to the full.

These observations, which anyone could verify, are enough to show that the problem of liberty, whether in itself or in relation to the Church, is by no means easy of solution. The answers that seem, on either side, most trenchant invite, of their very nature, the most subtle distinctions.

First, it must be noticed that the tendency, within the Church, to equate the Church with authority, and to oppose it to liberty, is of quite recent origin. It arose, indeed, at the time of the Renaissance and the Reformation, but was clearly formulated only after the Revolution.

Much is made of the mediaeval Inquisition; but it is too often forgotten that it was mainly the work of temporal rulers, encouraged perhaps by idealists of no official status, though these, unfortunately, included religious whose minds dwelt wholly in heaven, but whose feet were not always on firm ground. As for ecclesiastical authority, it was far more concerned to moderate the activities of the Inquisition than to encourage them. Alexander VI, not the most zealous of Popes, had the merit and the courage to inhibit the ferocity of the Most Christian and the Most Catholic kings; and, when his son, Caesar Borgia, wished to set up a strict censorship in Rome, he answered that at Rome everyone had always said just what he thought, and the Pope could not stop it, even if he wanted to.

No doubt, Paul IV thought and acted quite differently. With Pius IV, however, a more balanced policy regulated the final prescriptions of the Tridentine Reform, despite what is only too often alleged by partial historians on either side, whether forerunners of modern anti-clericals, like Paolo Sarpi, or early integralists, like Pallavicini.

But we need not delve into history to show that authority in the Church is less extreme in its claims than some of its protagonists would have it. We ourselves heard, a short time ago, an official closely associated with the highest teaching authority in the Church saying that the true Roman tradition in this matter was no less collegiate than monarchic; that, as a general rule, the supreme authority never decided anything without it being freely prepared and discussed beforehand in meetings of experts, equally competent, but seldom, at the outset, unanimous.

Instead, some persons, quite inappropriately, try to make the obedience of faith a particular instance of what, in general, is now known as the Führerprinzip —the principle which is a pure negation of liberty, of unconditional submission to an authority which decides, not only without appeal, but without previous discussion, which has no need to seek information, or to reckon with anything outside itself.

This idea of authority is not, by any means, the creation of the Church, but arose in civil society, at various times, as a simple by-product by natural reaction of a liberty degenerated into licence. The liberty of 1789, which believed itself to have achieved total liberation even from paternal authority, since it gave literal effect to the impulse to father-killing so well analysed later by depth-psychology—it was this liberty that gave rise inevitably to a Napoleon, and later to Hitler and Stalin.

For a time, it is true, this mistaken idea was upheld by both the civil authority proceeding from demagogy, or contaminated by it, and by religious thinkers. The

latter hailed it as the natural support of that specially
rigid order that, by necessary reaction, follows on a
period of upheaval. But it could not last long, any more
than did the honeymoon of the Napoleonic Concordat
and the 'Génie du Christianisme'. The 'black cardinals'
themselves, if they were to remain faithful to the religious authority, had very soon to set an example of
defiance of the authority of 'order'. At a later date, we
see the national-socialist authority, in the course of
establishing its position, proclaiming its intention to
base itself on what it called 'positive Christianity'.
Though the epithet was left unexplained, it attracted
the support of some, both among ecclesiastics and lay
exponents of Catholic action, until the swift sequence of
events made explanation unnecessary.

All this may serve us as a preparation for what we
ourselves may experience in the near future, for what
many of our brethren in countries not very far distant
already experience now. I mean that, however indis-
posed to do so at present, we may be compelled, sooner
or later, to recognise that true loyalty to genuine
religious authority is not synonymous with a passive
obedience that entails submission to all authority of
whatever kind. What we must be on our guard against
is an attitude of unthinking conservatism, or a simple
reflex of reaction, the outcome of the disorders of the
16th and the end of the 18th centuries, that seems to
have led only too many Christians, and clerics in
particular, to look on every successful dictator as sent
by Providence.

On the other side of the scale we see Christians, particularly numerous today, who extol liberty to such a

degree that they consider the ideas of authority, dependence and obedience to represent what is at best a necessary evil, or a transitional phase the sooner done with the better.

So it is that, both for these and those diametrically opposed to them, the idea of authority is a denial of liberty, and the protagonist of liberty must necessarily reject authority, or, if he is cautious, at least evade it. The latter is restive against paternalism in the Church; and maintains that, if the Church is, as she claims to be, the great educator of mankind, she ought certainly to be able to grasp what modern psychologists are at such pains to bring home to all concerned with education, that parents, if they are true to their calling, should not prevent but foster the growth of their children to maturity, and, in consequence, we are told, to their emancipation from all tutelage.

The logical consequence of such an attitude leads beyond rejecting the yoke of the Church to the refusal to admit any dependence at all in the religious sphere. In this connection, it is interesting to notice how many modern Christian thinkers are drawn to Feuerbach's criticism of religion, in some ways anticipating that of Marx, and are disquieted in conscience about it. It is well known that Feuerbach held that man could not be fully himself so long as he remained oppressed by the idea of God and the inevitable dependence this implied. Man's conscience, therefore, could never reach maturity till it should finally reject the idea of a divinity which necessarily confines and limits him. It may well seem strange that Christians should feel the fascination of this kind of argument, but it is undoubtedly the case that there are many today who do. If they desire to salvage the idea of God in spite of all, they are prepared to jettison all that lends itself to Feuerbach's criticism. In the previous section, we cited the strange contention of a Christian thinker who set himself up as a philosopher, and, maybe, thought himself a theologian. He wrote to a lady, whom one would have thought not especially qualified to receive his confidence, that the notion of the fatherhood of God was only a survival from the neolithic age. We are to understand by that the God modern man needs cannot be one prior to him, like a first mover on which his whole being depends; rather man must see him as that to which he moves forward, like the point omega that man's free creative activity is to attain in an absolute autonomy.

Others, whose metaphysic is a trifle less crude, explain that, in acknowledging the divine transcendence, we should rule out, as mythical elements, all that implies compulsion on us, or any kind of intervention on the part of God. For such a philosopher of religion as M. Henri Duméry says, 'If it is normal, or obligatory, to place God at the source of all, it is necessary to add that he is not its author in the same way as man is of what he produces'.

Likewise, he goes on to say, 'revelation is a human structure, but its origin is divine inasmuch as *it expresses the presence of God in the Spirit who utters this presence*'—this latter phrase is underlined for our benefit, to prevent us being misled by a respectful or cautious ambiguity in terms.

What this means, if it means anything at all, is that, if we must still speak, as everyone does, of the incarnation of God in man, we are to understand by it simply the unbounded achievement of the human consciousness in that supreme projection of itself that it calls God, —just as, by creation, we are to understand, not an action of which God is strictly speaking the author, but a paradoxical characteristic of the highest kind of consciousness of self and the world attainable by man in the transcending (the Hegelian Aufhebung) of our inevitable finiteness, at the very instant we recognise it.

It is time that these conflicting dialectics, authoritarian and libertarian, ceased to occupy in turn the stage of Christian thought, each thrusting the other into the background, but ever reproducing the same simpliste turn of thought, though of opposite tendency.

St Paul himself was aware of the theme of man's loss of liberty, and he had a dialectic of his own, which, however, was not that of master and slave, but—and the difference is significant—of slave and free man as such.

St Paul teaches that man is, indeed, called to liberty, but to a liberty which he qualifies, in a most revealing way, as 'the liberty of the children of God'. For the time being, he has forfeited this liberty. Man was made for 'the liberty of the children of God', yet he was born, not free, but enslaved, enslaved to a hostile power. This power, in some ways, transcends him, is outside his reach, being the power of Satan; but, in another way, his chains are of his own making, his enslavement he himself brought about. The power of Satan over man is no other than the power of his own sinfulness, the power of the passions and concupiscences.

All this amounts to saying that the source of our present loss of freedom is to be found in the confusion between freedom and autonomy at the very beginning. In that, precisely, consists the first sin; it was the refusal, on the part of created liberty, to depend on any thing or person, more particularly on Him who is the Father of all liberty, namely God.

Through his refusal to accept the law of the Spirit, though this was also the inner law of man—that is to say, although God's command was in accord with the deepest tendency of the human heart—man became subject to what St Paul calls 'the law of the members', a law of disorder, inner disintegration, which delivers us over to that domination of the 'flesh' and the 'world', of which we spoke previously, and which is the servitude in which Satan keeps captive the whole of creation, when it thinks itself liberated from its Creator.

Man, then, being in this condition, what does God do? The Son of God, pre-eminently free himself, makes himself voluntarily a slave in order to redeem those who are slaves. He is born òf a woman, born under the law, to deliver those who are under the law. No one takes away his life; he has received of the Father full power to dispose of it, and he gives it freely, out of love, just as the Father himself so loved the world that he gave his only son, that whoever believed in him might not perish, but might have eternal life. Man had been destined to liberty, because he had been made to the image of God; but now we see this very Image to which he had been made, the living Image of the Father, who, far from exploiting his equality with God, strips himself of it, empties himself, and takes on the condition of man, the status of a slave, becoming obedient, obedient unto death, even the death of the Cross. We see, too, this humiliation, freely undergone, this humiliation of a love voluntarily obedient, breaking all the bonds of slavery. Not only is Christ, after his humiliation, by the very fact of his humiliation, supremely exalted, but, raised up on the Cross, raised up into heaven, he draws all men to himself. To those who follow him, who take up and carry their cross after him, he communicates liberty, the royal liberty of the children of God. As the apostle says, Christ has delivered us that we may be free, 'stand fast and be not held again under the yoke of bondage' (*Gal.*, v. 1).

At the same time, St Paul exhorts his followers to 'serve the Lord Christ' (*Col.*, iii. 24), to become 'servants to God' (*Rom.*, vi. 22), making it clear that such servitude is identical with deliverance from slavery to sin. He goes further still, saying: 'Whereas I was free as to all, I made myself the servant of all' (1 *Cor.*, ix, 19), and encourages his disciples 'by the charity of the Spirit to serve one another' (*Gal.* v. 13). These words, 'by charity', give us the key to the whole problem.

What caused our enslavement, the primordial servitude from which all oppression takes its rise, is that false liberty, that pretension to autonomy which rejects the dependence of love, of filial love corresponding to what is paternal love *par excellence*, the Love of God. To break the bond of enslavement to sin, to restore the true liberty of the creature, the liberty of the children of God, the love of God went to the extreme of making itself a slave, a slave, in fact, of its entire liberty to love. This paradoxical dependence, freely assumed, of the Creator himself on his creature, results in freeing the latter from all his bonds, from Satan, sin, the flesh, the world, even from death. But, once regained, this liberty could continue in being only as a state of dependence, joyfully accepted, by which love responds to love.

In the condition of slavery in which we were found by the love of the Father in his only Son, it is our very acceptance of that state that delivers us. Poverty, suffering and death are the product of our false autonomy, of the oppression which our perverted liberty turned into. But poverty, suffering and death are now the indispensable means of the purification of our recovered liberty. Our greedy pretence to own ourselves had as sole result the loss of ourselves; but the loss of ourselves has become the means of freeing us from self, our supreme enemy, to hand us over to love, which alone is true liberty.

For to be free as God is free means, not confining oneself in egoism, but opening oneself to love. Liberation from our servitude means reopening ourselves to his love, delivering ourselves to its infinite generosity, and so, in the words of St Paul, becoming 'freedmen of Christ' or 'slaves of Christ'. Becoming 'servants of God' and 'servants of all' is one and the same thing, for we cannot love God without loving all that he loves, we cannot love God without making ourselves, with Christ, all things to all men.

What results from all this is that man is not yet free; he has to become free, or rather regain freedom. For him, to be free and to be to the image of God is the same. Consequently, to be free is, in a sense, primarily to be dependent, to obey. It means to depend on God, to obey him, in order to learn from him how to

D

experience that royal liberty which can only be fulfilled in his infinitely generous love.

To redeem us, the Son of God became man and willed to learn what obedience was, and so, for our part, we have to relearn it after him, in the setting of our human life which he chose to share. His own obedience to the loving plan of his Father made him obedient to men, first of all to those given him by God as his parents on earth, however below him personally, later to all men, evil men included. In this way there was wrought in him, and by him, in our human nature, that obedience to the Spirit which is one with true liberty, the perfection of love.

That is the way we, too, have to follow. We attain to true liberty, not by rejecting all authority, but by obedience, even to death. At the same time, no authority should have any other aim than to develop in us the liberty of the children of God.

William of St Thierry worked out, better perhaps than any other spiritual writer, this dialectic of obedience which is also that of true liberty.

Man, he says, dominated by the passions of the flesh and blind to his real good, must begin by practising, in pure faith, what he calls the obedience of necessity, that is to say an obedience whereby he abandons himself wholly to those to whom Christ has given authority in the Church, to lead us to the truth. But, by the very fact of exercising this faith, in his practice of obedience the Christian will gradually come to an increasing understanding of the faith. Along with this, his obedience, from being simply passive, docile indeed but in a way constrained, will become more interiorised and devoted; instead of obeying blindly, he will do so because he understands, ever more fully, the significance of obedience. He will proceed from mere obedience of necessity to the obedience of charity. That does not mean that he will be less obedient, but more. He will obey his lawful superiors better than before, because he will obey them, not only with all his strength, but with his whole heart. No doubt, at this stage, he will distinguish more clearly the human qualities of those Christ has placed over him from the function entrusted to them; and, as a result, will meet with difficulties in obeying which he had not previously, when still incapable of reflection. By the very fact that he has become capable of judging the things of God, he will have, not only the right, but the duty, of bringing to the notice of his superiors aspects of reality he thinks himself to perceive which they, being human, may not have noticed or have neglected. But, once he has done this and used all rightful means for the purpose, he will, if his progress in the way of faith and obedience, and so of real liberty, is genuine, accept in the end, without complaint, the decision of authority. He will do so, even though actually unable to see its justification. He will abide by it even if he cannot help considering it positively bad, provided, of course, that it does not entail sin for him, for the supreme authority for the Christian is always that of conscience, and no other can dispense him from following it. Yet conscience itself, when it has reached the level clearness of what we have called the obedience of charity impels man to obey unjust superiors, if they be so, equally with the just, so long as they do not infringe the limits of their authority. At this level, in fact, we are drawn to obey, not only our superiors in religion, but our brethren too without exception. Progress in faith, accompanied by that of charity, uproots our inveterate conviction that our judgment is necessarily truer than that of anyone else, and so forms in us a disposition to true humility, which welcomes all truth, whatever its source.

Only in this way can the obedience of charity pass over, in its turn, to a true union of the spirit with God. When this takes place, the Christian comes to experience full and complete liberty, but only because then the Spirit of God governs him directly without intermediary. Nevertheless, those whom the Spirit so governs, precisely because they are free, and can no more be enslaved by any person or thing, become, in the fullness of their love, the slaves of all. Immune, as they are, from all deception and illusion, they are without any possible liability to rebel, for they have passed beyond the range of any conceivable conflict. Not only do they obey, with childlike trust and openness, the superiors who stand in the place of Christ, not only do they make themselves the servants of their brethren, but the servants of all. They allow themselves to be exploited by all without repining; yet, it is they who are now the guides of the world—its destiny is in their hands in spite of all the wise and powerful men of this world, whoever they be. What appears to human eyes the reign of man and his pride is, to the eye of faith, what the Apocalypse calls, 'the reign of God and his saints'.

IV

INTELLECT AND FAITH

OPINIONS on the function of the intellect in the Church are, perhaps, even more at variance with one another than those taken up, either within the Church or on its behalf, on the question of liberty. Of course, all the Messieurs Homais, the Bouvarts and Pécuchets, by tradition the great defenders in France, disinterested ones naturally, of thought with a capital T, see the Church as the stronghold of obscurantism. Against their attacks, Catholics vainly brandish the names of St Augustine, St Thomas, Pascal and Newman, or, less convincing but of wider appeal, those of Pasteur or Branly.

When, however, we consider the fate of human thought in certain countries which flatter themselves at having finally escaped that religious alienation denounced by Feuerbach, when we see how various dogmatisms, how many stifling assumptions, claim to control, not only the sciences of man, but the physical sciences as well, it is quite out of the question to hold that nowadays religious belief, in particular the Catholic faith, is the greatest obstacle to intellectual progress.

The conflict, or at least the tension, between intellectualism and anti-intellectualism is at its highest within the Church itself. As on the question of liberty, we find

two opposing factions: the modernists, by very definition, are for the intellect, the integrists, against. In this
matter, however, much more directly than in the question of liberty, it is evident that the opposition is not so
much the concern of two distinct parties. Everyone is
conscious of a division within himself; even the Christian schools that feel themselves most committed to one
side or other are, in reality, at variance, in their
members, as to the actual or rightful place of thought
in Christianity.

Let us take the integrist position. No doubt, it regards
as captious the distinction between liberty of thinking
and free thought. It accepts only truths given from
above and likes to see them propounded with suitable
measures of coercion. Yet we find its upholders are the
most enamoured of a purely rational apologetic, and
maintaining, as a truth of faith, that assent to revelation
must be given initially independently of any influence
proceeding from the light of faith. The *Journal* of
Charles du Bos, now in course of publication, throws a
vivid light on the mentality that may result from principles of this kind. This unfortunate man, an *anima
naturaliter Christiana*, in some ways a congenital Augus-
tinian, on reaching the harbour of faith, found himself
welcomed by certain formidable good Samaritans, and
was soon the object of their persecution. His offence
was that he persisted in holding that God and his grace
had some part in the action of the mind which sought,
but had not yet found, him. What a strange inconsist-
ency in those who know no other final principle but
that of authority, and yet could not admit the genuine-
ness of a faith reached otherwise than by solitary logical

deduction which should find the God of the Gospel in the conclusion of a syllogism!

It would, however, be erroneous to think that contradictions of this kind were confined to one school of thought. One who upholds the necessity of critical, rational and positive thought tells us that 'the dogmatic theologian, the exegete, the patrologist, the historian of doctrines, in general all the specialists in the sciences of religion, who, jumbling up methods and subject-matter, aim at being both believers and savants, but believers with a learned faith and learned with an uncritical science, all these are but concordists and eclectics; specialists in compromise, professors in one half of their minds, they ply a dubious trade. The logician has the duty of exposing their duplicity, which is an insult to faith and a disgrace to science'. But this is simply to make of faith something wholly irrational, to confuse transcendence with complete inexpressibility. More curious still, the upholders of reason often foist on texts interpretations they cannot bear, or even assume facts instead of investigating them, in order to maintain or, at least, not to disturb, a theory held to be wholly positive and rational.

What conclusion is to be drawn? That man, especially the thinker, whether Christian or not, is a strangely inconsequential being? That is undoubtedly true, but not the whole of the truth. It is still more true that there is no truth, of any kind at all, that can, without stultifying itself, emancipate itself from all that is not itself. This particularly applies to thought in the Christian sphere; and, for this very reason, it is here more than elsewhere that it can come to perceive the requirements, seemingly opposed, but really complementary, of its true development.

Let us consider more closely the double temptation which besets all Christian thinking. It finds itself caught in the toils of concordism or of what is called the double truth. The former supposes that revealed and rational truth are so closely allied that they both say the same thing in different words. But, to support this, it manipulates the data of revelation in such a way as to distort them utterly. At the same time, it erects a structure of false science, whose tenets, reached by deductive reason and experience, are made to fit in with the ready-made formulas held to be deduced from revelation. In this way, the six days of Genesis become geological periods, and that the serpent crawls on its belly as a result of God's curse is confirmed by the observation on its skeleton of tell-tale excrescences which could easily be the remains of small feet miraculously vanished.

The highest peak in this range of reasoning is the assurance that Adam, though he lacked, for good reason, the umbilical cord, must have had the vestige of one so that his human nature would be perfect, not to mention the theory of the Creator hiding fictitious fossils in the geological strata to deceive, in our day, the calculations of unholy scientists.

The theory of the double truth leads to equally strange consequences. Thinkers at the opposite pole to concordism are perfectly willing to affirm, Sunday by Sunday, their belief in God the Father Almighty, Creator of heaven and earth, of all things visible and invisible, while holding, all the same, that the visible world has always existed, and that, as to the invisible world, it is a conception alien to Christianity, brought into Judaism from Persia and now, of course, to be rejected. Or they maintain that Christianity is wholly grounded on faith in Christ's resurrection, while, at the same time, they give out that the account of the empty tomb is obviously just a legend, and that, in any case, to ascribe to it any importance is the sign of a mentality arrested at the mythological stage.

However, it is easier to poke fun at these inconsistencies than to avoid them. We are all, to some extent, concordists, and that does not prevent us from floundering about, more or less skilfully, in the no man's land between science and revelation.

Must we, then, surrender to the modern non-Christian thinker who points out to us the pitiable compromises and absurd contraditions into which faith leads us when we start to reflect? By no means; first, because the non-Christian himself is in the same predicament, and, next, because, for the Christian, the problem is not insoluble, though the solution may not be immediately obvious.

The fact is that, in every sphere of human knowledge, the deeper we penetrate the harder it is to harmonise our conclusions with those of other disciplines. Consequently, the specialist is always tempted, either to confine himself so closely to his own subject that he ignores of set purpose, if he does not deny, the existence of others, or else to apply his own special terminology to subjects for which it is unsuitable. Even in the sciences, like physics and mathematics, whose advance in modern times has been so closely connected, the processes of discovery and reasoning are so different that the revision of concepts, so necessary to the progress of science, never quite catches up with its needs. It is well known that Einstein, towards the end of his life, was baffled by his inability to unify his conception of the physical universe, because he could express his discoveries only in the current mathematical language, while, at the same time, the mathematicians admitted they were unable to find a formula incorporating all Einstein's data. A little while ago, the scientific world was excited by the hope that Heisenberg, who had proved the impossibility of ascertaining exactly either the position or the speed of ultimate particles, had now discovered a formula to restore to our conception of the world the unity which the very progress of our knowledge had impaired.

If such a divergence has arisen, and the hope of agreement so long disappointed, in the case of the two sciences that, since Descartes, have been so closely allied, and whose co-ordination lies at the base of all modern technology, what can we expect of other branches of knowledge whose mutual relations are quite different?

As regards psychology, we have only just begun, in France, to recover from a state of paralysis in investigation, caused by the tyranny of a concordism undoubtedly worse than the most irrational of theologians have ever sought to impose. Dominated by the assumptions of a purely materialistic explanation of mental data, and, in consequence, chained to an exclusively organic etiology of mental disease, psychiatry in France has gone to desperate lengths in keeping up a barrier against psychoanalysis and other forms of analytical psychology. It was held that any medical science worthy of the name should either ignore psychology altogether, as a simple epiphenomenon without any reality of its own, to be left

to the purveyors of literature and poetry—those specialists in vagueness, in the words of Aldous Huxley—
scientifically scarcely more respectable than priests;
or else it should reduce psychological factors to the
mechanisms of the brain and nervous system. In other
words, it was a choice between the double truth and
concordism. In the end, in France as elsewhere, depth-
psychology succeeded in breaking through; but, since
official science had declined, as long as it could, to recognise it, there is great danger of it falling into the hands
of charlatans, and so of degenerating into a new
mythology.

The fact is that science, as much as faith, is menaced
by concordism and double truth. This is nowhere more
clearly shown than by the attempts of some German
historians and exegetes, followers of Rudolf Bultmann,
to demythologise Christianity.

Bultmann himself began by putting himself forward,
in perfect sincerity, as a disciple of Karl Barth. The
latter was rightly annoyed with the 'scientism' that had
taken over scriptural exegesis and the historical critique
of Christian origins, in German Protestant circles before
the 1914 war; and so he desired to restore a theological
mode of exegesis, and a theology which would be something more than a mere account of successive systems.
But Barth thought this could be done by simply throw-
ing over the intellectual world of nineteenth-century
German religious philosophy, rather than by introduc-
ing modifications into it. This world was formed
entirely on the Kantian opposition between reality in
so far as it could be apprehended, wholly immanently,
by man, and reality as in itself transcending human

knowledge and subjectivity. Barth, in reaction to this, proclaimed the God who reveals himself as pre-eminently transcendent; but, at the outset at least, he failed to see that this revelation of the hidden God could present him otherwise than as essentially hidden, inaccessible to human thought, and beyond any analogy with what falls within the scope of our senses or intellect.

Bultmann, as a thinker anxious to remain a Christian as well, declared himself enthusiastically for this point of view; for it seemed to leave the exegete and the historian of Christian origins full autonomy in their spheres, without their faith being affected in any way.

It is to the credit both of Bultmann and Barth that neither could long remain satisfied with a solution of the problem which, in fact, simply suppressed it. Nevertheless, whereas Barth came, without being fully aware of it, more and more into line with the methods of traditional theology, Bultmann changed over from his theology of double truth to what was really one of concordism, which resulted, not from theological indolence, but, as in other cases, from a science trespassing outside its proper sphere.

Piecing out, with a philosophical naïveté common to so many scholars, the general structure of a mental universe which he held to be the only one compatible with modern science, Bultmann rejected, as pure mythology, all the elements in the apostolic teaching which did not agree with it; in particular, he excluded whatever presupposes any divine intervention in the course of events, the interference of any sort of 'spirit' in the material world. Christ is no longer the bearer and object of the 'kerygma', the 'good news of salvation', except as he is actually the occasion of our becoming aware of the paradoxical relation between God and man by the very nature of things—the nothingness of man who relies on himself, the joyful assurance of man when he puts his trust in the reality which wholly transcends him, but outside of which he is nothing. Much might be said in criticism of this account of the essence of Christianity, which rejects so much that the Church has always believed to be part of it, and, by a marvellous stroke of pre-established harmony, coincides with the central theme of Heidegger's existentialism, adjusted slightly to a vaguely pietistic terminology. Here we shall just recall a twofold observation of Jaspers, a philosopher and psychologist who is no fonder than Bultmann of ecclesiastical dogma, but whose logic is far more trenchant. Bultmann, he says, on the one hand extrapolates, quite unjustifiably, the methodological criteria of the physical and historical sciences, mixing them up with little regard for their disparities in order to construct a mental picture of the universe. Thus, postulates verifiable only in a restricted sphere become axioms totally unverifiable on which the whole of reality is built up *a priori*. As a result, Bultmann, ignoring the progress made by ethnology, the history of religions, and depth-psychology for the last twenty years, supposes a myth to be just a childlike conception, whereas the whole tendency of the human sciences nowadays is to rediscover the truth certainly underlying what the nineteenth century simply dismissed as 'mythological'. Bultmann therefore discards a caricature of a religious universe he had substituted for the reality, but set up in its place a mental universe with no other claim to be scientific than a terminology void of meaning because taken out of the only context to which it applies.

To Jasper's criticism of Bultmann, the historian of religions—before giving place to the theologian—might add an objection *ad hominem*, unforeseen indeed by Bultmann, but one which turns his whole system against him. Mythology, as it is found in the most various religions of mankind, and also detected in the depths of human psychology in all ages, seems more and more clearly to be characterised by a projection, in terms of human history, of certain archetypes, independent of time, that everyone bears within himself, and which represent his permanent relationship with the universe. Consequently, what Bultmann regards as the essence of a Christianity purged of myth, that is to say a non-temporal relationship between man and the whole of reality projected into the history of Christ (whatever this history actually was), this so-called demythologised Christianity is, in fact, simple myth in its pure state, and, what is more, robbed of its living force by the process of abstraction.

Bultmann completely failed to see that the mystery underlying the Christian faith is something quite different. This mystery, so wonderfully described by St Paul at the beginning of the first epistle to the Corinthians, is by no means to be equated with the myths common to all the religions of mankind, something corresponding to the deepest instincts of human mentality, a mere intuitive projection of the most abiding laws of life in the actual world. The Christian mystery, the mystery of faith, is not just another version of a figurative story exemplifying the perennial history of man, but the affirmation of a unique event, absolutely unparalleled, which *ultimately brings about a change in the perennial history*; for it represents, or rather brings about, a cleavage in the apparent course of events, by which the Creator's direct action in the world will, finally, bring to its appointed term a history which, otherwise, would merely repeat itself indefinitely.

The proclamation of the mystery, as made by St Paul, is what guards us against the illusion of a double truth and, at the same time, enables us to avoid any kind of concordism.

The mystery for St. Paul is, in fact, the great secret of the divine wisdom, which alone holds all the strands of reality and alone is able to bring them together by means of what had never entered, or could enter, the heart of man, but what God has revealed to him and entrusted to him.

Man, of himself, cannot attain to a coherent view of the whole of reality; for, on the one hand, he cannot abstract himself from reality to embrace it in a single view, and, furthermore, reality, in its actual state, is fundamentally disintegrated, and no human or cosmic power can restore it.

All that man can do, in forming a view of the world, is to join together, more or less imperfectly, his views, necessarily partial and extremely defective, on parts of an immense universe whose various sectors he explores in turn. Nor can he ever exhaust any one of these sectors; moreover, there is no standpoint available from which he can view the whole at once. The price he has to pay for his limited successes in one field is a specialisation which tends to unfit him for other fields he has to neglect in exploring the first.

In particular, the marked success of modern science in the domains of physics and chemistry has resulted in a tendency for our perceptions in other fields to become atrophied. The engineer has achieved outstanding successes, but a man who confines himself, by choice or necessity, to engineering closes his mind to the religious view of the universe to the point of believing that such a view does not exist at all or else is illusory. In addition, he incurs the risk of complete failure in the spheres of aesthetics, human relations, and in the moral side of life, either through disregarding them altogether, or through denying their own special character, seeking, for instance, to reduce his relations as manager with workers, of husband with wife, of father with his children, to the terms of an equation.

Even if the specialist were capable, as some extraordinary geniuses like Leibnitz were, of being an expert in every field, there is no one who could possibly reach the point of grasping the whole universe in one sweep of vision. This would entail stepping out of the universe, and placing himself at the centre from which all depends; in other words, he would have to be God.

Furthermore, what the Word of God makes known to us is in perfect accord with one of man's most persistent intimations, namely, that there is, in the actual universe, in physical as well as human nature, something disjointed, and this tries to repair itself, but is unable to succeed. So, then, even for God, the unification of all things in a comprehensive view is not just a question of looking at them from an eminence; it is a work that has to be undertaken and achieved, in fact, it is the greatest work of all.

Does it follow that the view of the whole to which we are fated to strive, and the unification of the universe in and for man to which all his activities are directed, are quite unattainable? The answer given by faith is that neither of these is beyond reach, but that neither can be had unless the key, the crux of all things, is put into our hands by God. In this consists precisely the mystery of the Christian faith, the mystery of Christ and his cross.

The mystery of faith, then, is not just a truth lacking all contact or bond with the truths our intellect can reach by itself. Nor is it a truth handed down, ready made, to replace, on their own level, the truths we could find out for ourselves. It is something to which all real investigation into partial truths is constantly tending, and apart from which is powerless to reach the truth of the whole. It is the creative truth which is alone capable of resolving the ultimate antinomies that oppress man more insistently as his knowledge gains in depth.

In the same way as the life of man reaches out, by an inescapable aspiration of his being, to the fullness of life in a perfect and absolute union of love, and yet is oppressed by the inevitability of death, so does his mind aspire to encompass the whole in a single unity, but, the further he advances, the more swiftly what he pursues seems to evade and elude his grasp.

Likewise, as man invariably tends, in the course of his life, to create an idyllic situation where an illusion of perfect love would make him indifferent to the course of events, and even oblivious of death, so, in the sphere

E

of thought, he tends to create for himself simplified models of the universe, which would account for everything in terms of one clear and distinct idea.

In his ardour for the limited truths he has managed to discover and for what they seem to promise to his continued activity, man comes up against the faith, and is tempted to reject it as an alien encumbrance. But it is faith which really enlightens his mind by reminding him of what the best elements in his own thinking tend to make him forget, namely, that there is more in this world than can be grasped by our thought.

Faith, true Christian faith, is a hindrance only to false science, false, either because, through indolence, confined to its present limits, or because unjustifiably extended beyond its proper sphere.

Science, when it is something more than a narrow self-contained pursuit, or a mere occupation long followed and despotic, the science that attains to true wisdom comes thereby to acknowledge the fact of mystery present in the world of things and of man.

Then it is that, so far from closing the eyes of man to revelation, to the mystery of faith, it actually prepares him for it. As Origen says, in a golden utterance taken as his motto by one of the greatest of modern apologists: 'Once we acknowledge by faith that the same God is the author of nature and of the Scriptures, we are no longer astonished to find mysteries in both.'

V

TRADITION AND RENEWAL

In the last section, we studied the problem of the relation between intellectual activity and the truths apprehended by faith. We confined ourselves, however, to a single aspect of the problem, often enough the only one envisaged, the relations between science and faith. In fact, there is a tendency to think that faith only meets with the action of the mind when outside itself, as it were. Historians of Christian thought often take as axiomatic that thought is an alien importation into Christianity, and assume that thought, within the Church, began only under the influence of hellenism. From this point of view, the history of Christian thought would be but the history of the hellenisation of Christianity.

Nothing could be more untrue. Neither in the Church, nor among the Jews, did the exercise of thought wait upon contact with the culture of Greece. The real truth is that there can be no faith without thought. Faith does not only, of its very nature, stimulate thought in the believer, but it has no existence apart from thought; it is itself an activity of the intellect.

This brings us to a problem which is no longer one of the understanding *and* faith, but one of the understanding *of* the faith.

There are, of course, those who hold that this kind of

understanding is purely passive. Whether for the faith or against it, they agree that faith and tradition are the same thing, that faith has to confine itself to accepting, just as they are, the deliverances of tradition, and anything further that results from the action of the individual mind only adulterates it.

At the opposite extreme are those who hold that faith is a leaven or ferment, that it is only alive in so far as it penetrates and activates, turn by turn, the various forms of autonomous thought that succeed one another in the world. Christian thought is, thus, inexhaustible in its fruits, though it possesses no distinctive form of its own. It is ever active, constantly at work, but it has no other function than to baptise, we are told, all the successive forms and varieties of human thought, rejecting none, and committed to none.

Each of these extremist positions rests on the assumption, which they take for granted without discussion, that we have already pointed out as fundamentally agnostic. To look upon any action of the intellect in matters of faith as nothing but a threat to the purity of tradition and a danger to faith, or else to confine its action to assimilating what has been discovered independently of faith—each of these attitudes assumes that faith, of itself, is no concern of the mind.

There could be no greater mistake than this. For it would admit, on the one hand, all those misconceptions which, claiming to preserve the purity of tradition, only serve to sterilise and petrify it, and, on the other, all those which, setting out to stimulate the development, or, as is still said, the progress of doctrine, finish by reducing Christian thought to the state of a chameleon, ceaselessly and exclusively occupied in taking on fresh colours according to the prevailing fashion.

The initial mistake about the intellect, from which proceeds the mistaken notion of faith we have pointed out, is that of looking on it as now passive, now active, whereas it is always both active and passive at the same time. The difference between the intellect within the sphere of faith and outside it is not the difference between the intellect in a passive state and the intellect exercising, or recovering, its natural mode of action. It is simply a matter of different modes of activity of the same intellect, according to the passivities, widely differing from one another, imposed on it by its various objects.

The idea of a wholly autonomous activity of the human mind, if taken strictly, is absolutely chimerical. The mind, in its search for truth, cannot be, in any real sense, independent; in fact, it is only by the strictest submission, the most perfect docility to reality, as this comes to it from outside, that it has any chance of reaching truth. In this process, it is not, by any means, autonomous; on the contrary, it is, is bound to be, delivered up to the interior dominance of reason, which takes us out of our own individuality, but which alone is able to lead us towards truth, precisely according as our ego refrains from interfering with the light which is in every man, but which transcends every man.

In this respect, the situation of the mind when confronted with supernatural revelation is no different from its situation over against findings that pertain wholly to the natural order. Or rather the difference in the two cases lies in the varying approach required of one and the same intellectual instrument by different objects. Yet this difference does not mean they have nothing in common, nor that the mind, in the sphere of revelation, finds the atmosphere alien. Both nature and grace are from God. It is in relation to the same God that we are passive when our activity is most intense, and by him, too, that we are active even in the depths of our passivities, whether we are engaged in the classification of natural objects or in opening our minds to the revelation which transcends the world of nature.

It has been very well said that always, and in both cases, God acts on us, and causes us to act, as if by the contact of those two fatherly hands of which St Irenaeus speaks, and which he saw at work both in the creation and in the redemption. Always God is acting on us by the hand which takes hold of us from the outside, and, through the sense-impressions coming from the world, sets on us, as it were, an imprint, and it is this which our minds have to strive to explore and assimilate completely, in their effort to understand the truth. Always, too, he is acting in us and causing us to act by the other hand which moves us unseen, in the deepest place of our being, and which is, as it were, the soul of our soul, being the light man bears within himself from birth, which, yet, is not his, and regarding which he should even now say: 'In *thy* light we shall see the light . . .' Whenever one of these hands is at work to form us, to make us into our true selves, the other is always acting in concert with it. There is nothing in the mind that is not first in the senses, except, as has been said, the mind itself; and all that we receive from the senses, as well as our whole mind, is from God. For that reason, to anyone who reflects, God is seen both behind the appearances of the world of sense and behind the activities of the mind, just as, antecedently to reflection, man seems to divine him as wholly transcendent—the God of heaven, as well as the God immanent in the deepest part of the soul, the God of conscience.

By the fact of revelation, this fundamental relation we have with God, in our intellectual activity, whether we are aware of it or not, whether we advert to it or not, is neither disturbed nor changed in its basic structure, which is derived from creation, the nature of the world and of ourselves. What happens is, simply, that it is drawn closer, and, at the same time, made more discernible.

What do we mean when we say that God speaks to us? We mean that, in the impressions the world makes on our senses, there are signs causing us, first to gain intimations of, then to perceive for certain, a personal action on the part of God, an approach, an intervention. But we can only recognise these signs in so far as the divine light in us becomes correspondingly vivid. This light always derives from the one God, the author of all minds, but it is not merely the reason he created in us that knows the world where he placed us, but the personal God who, in us, knows the personal God coming into the world. The Spirit of God, coming down into man, perceives the processes in the world whereby the Son of God prepares to become man. And once the Son of God, become man, has risen and, in his person, transfigured the world, the Spirit of God, in us, testifying that 'this Jesus, whom you crucified, God has raised from the dead', will, likewise, testify to our own spirit that we are now the sons of God.

It is always the same hands of God which mould us in the course of events. At one time, they let themselves be simply divined, without being distinctly recognised. Now, however, they come together, and, as it were, grasp one another, in the world and within us, and so become clear to our sight.

This is the standpoint from which we should come to understand the gradual approach of faith, our accession to it, and the development of the life of faith. There is, then, no difficulty in seeing that the activity of the human mind, so far from being inversely proportional to its passivity under the hands of God, develops and expands in the degree it surrenders to it.

The Bible proclaims Abraham as the Father of all believers. In other words, with him the light of faith begins to dawn. It should be observed that this dawn seems to synchronise with the dawning of human intelligence. Yet faith and intelligence seem, at first, to be opposed. But looking more closely, we find the intellect, in seeming to surrender to faith, is set thereby on the way to true freedom, while, in rejecting faith, it becomes imprisoned and petrified.

Abraham appeared at the same moment as the first beginnings of Mediterranean civilisation. He came from Mesopotamia, where the first great empires were starting to form. For the first time, perhaps, a human society was set up which transcended the primitive tribe or clan. A state came into being, with a king as its head and centre of cohesion. It was a world of its own, made by man for his own sake, of which a man was the god.

This world of man, the city, was bound up with the universe by its possession of a holy place; but here the God of the cosmos was not so much worshipped as held in subjection for the benefit of man, for the king, by whose wisdom a human stamp was to be imprinted on his world. This city was both the product of the awakened intelligence of man and the stronghold where it established itself as undisputed master. But it could be also its prison; for the mind of man, from then on, was turned and fixed in the direction of an attempt to dominate the world, the gods included. All was to be brought in subjection to the will of man. He was, by his intelligence, to make the world *his* world, the world of his own schemes and, principally, of his appetites, those of pleasure, dominion and pride.

It looked as if all men were about to engage on this enterprise, conforming to this kind of wisdom which was embodied in the city of its planning; but there was one who refused to take part in it, who purposely withdrew. Abraham acted according to his belief in the promise made to him, and, as a result of obeying the command to go out and live apart, a new people was born. But this people, as yet in its infancy, was again mingled with one of those peoples in which the mind of man was at work to mould the world to his own purposes; and the only result of its ancestor's, Abraham's, departure was its falling into slavery to the Egyptians. Moses, however, came on the scene, and, though he could simply have adopted the wisdom of Egypt, a mysterious instinct made him prefer to all its treasures, whether of the mind or material wealth, the reproach of the people of God. He, too, was irresistibly drawn to the desert, and soon he took with him there the entire people, descended from Abraham. Then there began to take shape a whole history of extraordinary events. A series of inexplicable happenings resulted in the formation of a people apart from all the rest. Side by side with this development, there was slowly built up, within this people, through the medium of a whole line of prophets, a body of inspired truths. The prophets, though always more and more opposed to the mass of the people, never isolated themselves from it. Their inspiration always appeared to spring from their contact with events concerning the whole people; and they gradually elucidated the significance of these events for the sake of the people themselves. So it was that God slowly formed and purified his people, continuing, and at the same time interiorising more and more, that segregation, that marking out of his own, which began with Abraham and Moses. A succession of trials, of alternate deliverances and oppressions, brought about a striking advance from the justice of Amos to the mercy of Osee, from this to Isaias's faith in the utter holiness of God, from the faith of Isaias to the confidence of Jeremias in the nearness of God who is yet the God of heaven, till it finally issued, with Ezechiel, in the conviction of the need to forgo his presence, to lose all, in order to find it again, to die in order to be reborn.

Meanwhile, Egypt and Assyria, followed by Babylon, continued to erect the imposing structures of their civilisations which was represented, for Israel, by the tower of Babel. They advanced in their own kind of wisdom, the grasp, by the mind, of a world becoming more and more humanised, together with the royal art of moulding the world into a city made for man. But the effect of this wisdom was, also, to involve man in hostilities on a scale corresponding with its advance. Israel, situated between these empires all the more hostile for being so much alike, seemed perfectly defenceless; and constantly yielded to the temptation to adopt the wisdom of its neighbours, and compete with them. But, though Israel might acquire the wisdom of Assyria or Egypt, profiting from their experiences and speculations, the divine Word, in the form of events bearing the seal of the divine intervention, came to upset it all, taking hold of it and giving it an unforeseen turn and a quite different meaning. The kingdom of Israel, introduced, as its wisdom was, in imitation of the foreign kingdoms, was destroyed in the catastrophe brought about by its worldly policy; and the people were left with the kingly rule of God, the only Wise. At this point, the chosen people were in a state to receive the mystery, the greatest secret of the divine Wisdom, which does not simply reject human wisdom, but seems at first to contradict it, and, in so doing, carries it to the point where it cannot go of itself.

In this succession of events, Israel, in so far as it was faithful to the demands of God, seemed foolish in comparison with the mundane wisdom of its neighbours; but God's own fidelity was to show, in the history of the people he made his own, in sacred history, that is, that the folly of God is wiser than the wisdom of the world.

At last there came on the scene he who is the incarnate Word of God. He appeared wholly lacking in human learning, but yet men felt that he had a knowledge of them of which they were quite incapable, and which drew them strongly to him; through him they came to a knowledge of God of which they could not say exactly whether it terrified or fascinated them. He revealed them to themselves. 'He told me all things whatsoever I have done', said the Samaritan woman to her neighbours. They came and heard him, and said to her: 'We now believe, not for thy saying, for we ourselves have heard him, and know that this is indeed the Saviour of the world'.

But even those who believed did not yet fully believe. Once again, for the divine Word to penetrate to their hearts through the hard crust of the world in which they were steeped and of the flesh of which they were composed, it was necessary that this Word should be embodied in an event, one, at first sight, wholly inexplicable and passing belief. 'The Son of man must be delivered up to the Gentiles, and be rejected and be killed, and, after three days, rise again'. But Peter, at these words, took him aside, and said: 'This shall not be'; and the man to whom Christ had just said that on him, the rock, he would build his Church heard this answer: 'Go behind me, Satan; thou art a scandal unto me, because thou savourest not the things that are of God, but the things that are of men'. So true it is that faith, however prepared may be the ground, cannot be born in us without a real death and rebirth, through which we must pass as did he in whom we are to believe.

So it was that he said, on the eve of his death: 'It is expedient for you that I go; for, if I go not, the Paraclete will not come to you, but, if I go, I will send him to you.' Once again, we see that the Word that makes itself heard, and even the Word made flesh and become visible, cannot be received unless there is, in the recipient, an interior echo in harmony with it. But such an echo, only 'the Spirit of God testifying to our spirit that we are the sons of God' is able to arouse within us. 'I have yet many things to speak to you,' Christ went on to say, 'but you cannot bear them now. But, when the Paraclete, the Spirit of truth, is come, he will teach you all truth.'

A few days later, Christ, the Word made flesh, had died and was risen; but his death had only served to overwhelm the ill-rooted faith of his disciples, and, at his resurrection, they were positively incapable of believing. Meanwhile, as two of them were talking on the way of all that had happened, he joined them. His appearance was that of a stranger; not only did they fail to recognise him as risen, they did not recognise him at all. To them, as indeed to the eyes of the flesh, he was simply another traveller, hurrying along with them to reach his destination before nightfall. But, when at last arrived, they saw him making again the well-known gesture, repeating the words of blessing. He broke bread for them, and, from then on, they did not see him any more. Even the familiar appearance, which hid him while revealing him, vanished, and there was left only the bread he had himself blessed and broken. But the Spirit was watching over them, and opened to them the meaning of his words, just as it had caused them to recognise him in the breaking of bread. They said then, one to the other: 'Was not our heart burning within us, whilst he spoke in the way and opened to us the Scriptures?'

From now on, the Spirit gives understanding of this mystery to those who receive the Gospel and contemplate the sacramental signs of the mystery—the mystery of the Cross, the mystery of Jesus, which is the great secret to which the whole scriptural revelation leads up, in which the intervention of God in the world nears its fulfilment, changing all that is in the world and, in the first place, our heart—the great secret, too, of human history and its wisdom which leads ultimately to sin and death, till death, destroying sin, destroys also itself.

At this final stage, the mind of man has to renounce itself, transcend itself, but, ultimately, will fulfil itself in faith, faith in the divine Word and in the truth once for all delivered by God to his saints, the apostles of his Son.

Does this mean that now, since the whole truth of God is given to us in him who is the way, the truth and the life, the mind of man has nothing more to do than keep intact 'the sacred deposit' of revelation?

This could scarcely be so, since, as we have just seen, the human mind was so constantly at work to prepare for and receive God's supreme truth once it were given, a truth it could never acquire of itself. God did not 'inspire' his prophets and apostles by withdrawing them from all human experience, or inhibiting reflection on it. He did so, in fact, by launching them on an experience far wider and deeper than that in which the rest of mankind had lost its bearings, but an experience no less human for all that. He inspired them by stirring them to meditate on this experience, and to exercise their minds on it with passionate intensity. It is certainly the case that the inspired character of the divine

Word demands that we go forward willingly to make contact with the mystery which every kind of human wisdom finally comes up against, however self-confident it may be, provided it does not degenerate into reverie and illusion—the mystery, that is, of iniquity, the mystery of sin and death. But the mystery of iniquity, now that the Word of God has taken flesh, is the mystery of the Cross; and the mystery of the Cross, being accomplished, brings the Spirit of God into our hearts, who makes us behold the glory of God in the Cross of Christ and confess the truth of his resurrection.

This itself constitutes a death and resurrection of our human understanding; and, so long as we are still in the dimness of faith, it is death that is the more immediately felt. However, if our faith is not just external to us, and we commit ourselves to the experience of the Cross, upheld by the Spirit of light and life, the dimness becomes illuminated. When a person is not content with believing, as it were from the outside, the truth of the Gospel, but is drawn, as a result of his meditation, to 'do' that truth, as St John expressed it, his faith, though without ceasing to be faith, becomes knowledge. It becomes a 'knowledge of God' which is, indeed, an intellectual experience—the highest, perhaps, we can have on this earth—but one which is not something detached from experience pure and simple, or rather from the total experience of the believer to whom God has united himself in the sacramental signs, in the interior, invisible pouring out of the grace they give, that he may himself be united to God in charity.

To anyone who loves God as God wills us to love him, that is as God alone can love, he makes himself known;

for, possessing the love which is proper to God, he experiences, in a sense, what in God is most divine. It is no longer he who lives, but God who lives in him. In other words, his real life remains hidden, with Christ, in God. But when Christ, his life, appears, he will appear also. What he will be then has not yet been made manifest; but he already knows that he will be like to God, for he will see him as he is.

Thus, the element of 'nescience' in the knowledge our intellect here attains to by faith is simply the beginning of the death it must undergo, so that it may come to a new life enabling it, ultimately to attain the knowledge that surpasses all knowledge. Even now, this knowledge possessed by the blessed, the knowledge proper to God himself, makes our ignorance more learned than any knowledge of merely human origin.

The knowledge of the mystery of Christ is the first dawn of that perfect knowledge in which we shall know as, from all eternity, we have been known.

All this is an account of what happened to the human mind in the history of the chosen people, drawn, as they were, to the supreme Truth, then taken hold of by it, and, finally, possessing it themselves. But, it may be readily understood, it can happen to each of us, provided we assimilate our minds to the minds of those whom God formed for himself by gradually opening them to the vision of faith. Once our intelligence, like that of Moses, has the wisdom to prefer the apparent reproach of the people of God to all the brittle treasures of Egypt, it will, in searching the Scriptures, attain to Christ. It will find him by living over again, in the Church, the ever-present history of those advances God makes to us, which alone can lead us to a knowledge neither distorted, nor arrested at any point. Furthermore, by reliving with Christ, ever present in the Church, his whole mystery, our understanding will gradually reach, on its own behalf, and also for the rest of mankind, the unique wisdom which takes into itself all human wisdom, correcting its errors, however, and opening the way to the highest knowledge of all precisely at the point where the human mind comes up against impenetrable darkness.

Wherein, actually, does the achievement of purely human wisdom consist, an achievement ever advancing, it may be, but whose continual progress serves only to bring out more clearly the paradox it cannot escape?

Pascal, combining Epictetus with Montaigne, points out the two elements ever present in human history, and ever contending, namely, the greatness and weakness of man—his weakness in the world which is never more striking than when he thinks himself on the point of mastering the world; his greatness in having, at last, almost within his grasp the power, not only of one or other product of its evolution, but its very principle —the weakness of man who obtains from his discoveries fresh powers of self-destruction, who, when he thinks himself lord of all, finds he is further than ever from being master of himself.

The Wisdom that is made fruitful by the divine Word, which ultimately is identical with the Word received, once and for all, by the apostles and handed down as such by the Church, this Wisdom, without ever changing, continually renews itself by the light it throws, through its own mystery, on the problem that to

F

human wisdom only seems ever more cruel, the more insistent it becomes.

The only way in which the wisdom of Babel can gratify and even surpass its wildest aspirations is by accepting what, at first sight, frustrates them utterly, namely, the mystery of the Cross which baffles the intellect to restore it in the end, as it afflicts mankind to bring it healing and salvation.

VI

ACTION AND CONTEMPLATION

THE meaning of history for man would seem to be the building up of a city, the moulding of the world for his own purposes, for history is basically the history of man, not only because it is about him, but because it is he who makes it, and in it he makes himself.

Today we are more alive to this than ever before, no doubt because, now more than ever, in the last generation or two more than in all that have gone before, we seem on the point of achievement. We see in actual progress what is called the 'planetisation' of human endeavour and the human race itself. For the first time in history, man seems to have succeeded in fully exploring the earth and its potentialities; he seems on the verge of unifying the whole race in a common organisation for which, in spite of the divergences which still remain, we are all working in unison. Already, too, he is moving beyond this phase to a complete conquest of the universe and a transcending of the boundaries of the earth, both in his mastery, by his mind and will, of the very elements of which matter is composed, and by freeing himself, as he seems about to do, from narrow spatial bounds to subdue the cosmos itself.

Everything, it seems, must now be subject to the mind and will of man. Life itself is, perhaps, on the point of giving up its secrets to our studies and experiments, and we are well on the way to penetrating the last reaches of our own psychic structure. Soon, surely, man will become the master of himself as well as of the universe.

In the immediate prospect of these, his wildest dreams, which are already beginning to turn into realities, how could man be expected to reserve even a small part of his efforts from the great work, the work of creating both himself and the world, to be achieved both by man and for him?

All estrangement, too, both between men themselves and between man and the world, seems about to be finally overcome by this achievement of creation. What else is the salvation of man and the world but the entry of man and the world, of the world through man and of man by his knowledge and dominance of the world, into the final, supreme phase of creative evolution?

In view of all this, and of the changes man has brought about in his own being, and which it only remains for him to perfect, all the old humanisms seem anachronistic. In a certain review, Christian indeed but very careful never to be other than up to date, a theologian of highly planetised mentality gave an account of an 'art of thinking' propounded by a Catholic philosopher. Although the latter was a specialist in the development, even the progress, of doctrine, yet, as in this sphere one is always liable to come across persons more developed and progressive than oneself, the philosopher found himself severely handled. What does it mean, said this new kind of theologian, to talk about an art of being docile to reality, of eliminating chimeras, of attaining tranquil contemplation of truth? . . . This old Greek and Latin humanism is quite valueless; it has

lost all contact with recent and irreversible developments in man, and, in any case, has only too long turned
Christians from their proper way, that of creative activity, to lure them into a barren contemplation. What
business have we nowadays with this cult of solitary
thought, this passion for silence and the individual?
Why don't you finish with this mentality of escape, which
brings with it a wholly passive kind of spirituality?
The twentieth century Christian has no use for ivory-
towers. His own idea of charity, which is the same as
St Paul's, is allied with the sense of history to draw him
away from his individual concerns and immerse him in
those of the multitude. His culture is not, nor should
be, a closeted one; not for him a life spent in perusing
antiquated volumes, or patiently covering pages with
erasions and revisions. He is, on the contrary, a man of
the radio, in continual contact with the whole outside
world. His medium is the visual image, and he cannot,
like Malebranche, shut himself up in a room with drawn
shutters in order to meditate, nor would he want to if
he could. The cinema and television set are always opening to him new windows on to the world. The cinerama
places him in a three-dimensional setting which appeals
both to eye and ear, and so gives him a depth of imagery
formerly lacking, a total presence in the world which
should lead him to modes of thinking hitherto inconceivable. Let us hear no more of the pseudo-Platonic or
Aristotelian ideal of the wise man, too long that of
the Christian thinker. The modern world agrees with
the pure teaching of the Gospel, freed at last from
its hellenistic disguise, to forbid the Christian thinker
to remain aloof any longer, wasting his time in sterile

contemplation. We need action, action which, of its own nature, arouses a mental vigour which turns thought confidently to the outside world, immersing itself therein the better to penetrate it, accepting it, taking it over to master it and bring it to perfection—this, ultimately, is the outlook the charity which is creative has to impart to our thinkers, and, in any case, the modern world gives them no choice.

What should be our reaction to this? Was it really a calamitous mistake for Christian thinkers down the ages to adopt and develop the whole Greek idea of the contemplative life? Is a humanism whose primary aim is to liberate us from the world and ourselves, to enable us to attain a supra-temporal truth and possess it, is it now to be held invalidated by modern developments and in conflict with the real nature of Christianity? We may well ask if the construction of the modern world by the new means at our disposal—more precisely, the liberation of man by the application of new techniques to the world and his own personality—is, in fact, so urgent and beneficial as to demand of a Christian his entire collaboration, so that he may not stand aside from it in the least without a feeling of guilt, and a consciousness that the Gospel he believes in supports the reproaches levelled at him by the rest of the world for his indifference and, it may be, his actual repugnance.

We will take the latter question first, for on our answer to this depends our answer to the others.

To begin with, we may discern a kind of hesitation or vacillation in the very ranks of the 'advanced' Christians. Some of them tell us that the values of contemplation, particularly in the sphere of worship or the sacred

sphere—in other words, adoration—should supplement
the values of action and creation. There is, without
doubt, something beyond human activity. Once man
has moulded the world for his own benefit, and become
the master of his destiny, he will have to see before him
some end which makes it all worth while, and this end,
at any rate the final end, can only be God. But, they go
on to say, if we are to keep this place for God, and to
have any chance of being listened to when we present
the Gospel to our fellow-men, we must be careful now
not to incur the reproach of turning them from their
present task by administering opiates. We must, in fact,
make their task our own, unreservedly and without
deviating. We must show that Christianity, far from
distracting us, still more from hindering us from applying ourselves to the common work, spurs us to it with
greater zeal and conviction than others. Only then can
we obtain the right, and the power, to bear witness to
Christ in a way that will carry conviction. In short, what
we have to do now is to humanise the world, precisely
in order to evangelise it effectively in the future.

Others, however, not without a certain restiveness
towards these views, sing quite a different tune. They
reject out of hand, as quite chimerical, the slogan,
'humanise first and evangelise after', as assuming that
these could be two distinct and successive processes.
True humanisation, whatever people may think, is, they
tell us, the only real form of evangelisation. Where,
asked a young priest, the other day, who had decided to
abandon his priestly functions for an indefinite period,
where is the mystical body in these days, the real com-
munion of true charity? In the Church, exhausted in the

impossible task of bolstering up a decayed structure? Is it not rather to be found in the proletarian society coming into being the world over, applying its fraternal zeal, its creative enthusiasm, to the prodigious tasks devised and made possible by scientific humanism? Not only are we to give it our unreserved support to safeguard the ultimate values of the spirit and of God, but it would be an insult to humanity, now that it is on the way to achieve its destiny, at last perceived, to suppose that it needs any increment of spirituality from an outside source. In fact, it is the Christians who have to learn from it, to merge themselves in it totally, to watch their Church and their religion disappear as finite and distinct realities, to be recovered more truly and completely fulfilled in the triumphal surge of a humanity breaking its own bonds in order to create, in the end, without external aid, the new man in a new world.

Such remarks cannot fail to evoke what Bernanos said about people who confuse the apostolate with apostasy. We must, however, be on our guard against opposing ideas so manifestly based on irrational sentiments by others, equally ungrounded and no less confused.

What is common to the two kinds of 'progressivists' is the assumption that the building up of the modern city is part and parcel of the building of the mystical body, whether conceived as an initial stage thereof or giving it its final completion.

It is strange that the advance of modern civilisation is viewed by many Christians in a wholly favourable light, while a number of non-Christians, more clear-sighted, are more and more apprehensive about its fundamental ambivalence. But it is even more difficult to understand how a Christian can so easily persuade himself either that the final perfection of the world will come about by natural means, or else that it is quite superfluous to bring into it a spirituality it does not already possess in its own right.

In the world now in travail, is it really the mystical body alone that is being built up, or just a big concentration camp? It is quite true that mankind today is coming to form a single whole in which each of its parts is conscious of its place; it is also true that, in spite of the divisions and enmities still apparent within it, it is working to form a single civilisation, a unified society. America and Russia may be at daggers drawn; but, if we wait a few more decades, till the Russians have had time to provide refrigerators and television-sets for all, and the Americans to perfect, together with their own inter-planetary 'investigators', the repression of anti-constitutional activities, and to bring to heel the intellectuals, both peoples will have come to be so much alike that a conflict between them would be meaningless. But what sort of condition will they have come to?

A mass-regimentation, in the general setting of standardised comfort and of propaganda by radio and television moulding everywhere alike a humanity engaged solely in the same cerebral and sexual activities—is this really leading up to the fullness of the mystical body, or even preparing the way for it? If anyone is of that opinion, he is the victim of a serious confusion between the rise of the masses and the reign of charity, between the stifling of individual men in an anonymous humanity and their free harmonisation with one another in the people of God.

We have to remember that the first beginnings of the people of God, of the return of humanity, dismembered by sin, to 'the gathering together into one of the children of God who were dispersed', took place when Abraham separated himself from the first Babels which were in course of being built. It is not any kind of mass-assemblage that can bring about the reuniting, in charity, of mankind split asunder by sin. The first step, on the contrary, must necessarily be to break up all those pretended integrations which crush the individual and never form a real unity; and, in the whole history of the building up of the body of Christ, the various processes of assimilation are genuine only when accompanied by a continual work of detachment. No doubt, it is the city of man, built by men, that is to provide the members of the city of God, and the latter has to address itself to men and understand them as formed by their own city; but, to incorporate them, it has to remake them, and we must not deceive ourselves by thinking that the city of God can possibly be equated with the city made by men.

Sometimes it happens, as at the time of Constantine, that the city of man itself expresses its wish to be incorporated in the city of God, to adopt its customs and laws. The city of God cannot simply repel such an advance, but it cannot accept it without creating for itself as it were refuges, places inaccessible to any earthly city, where it can live again according to the full rigour of what God demands. The alliance, in the Constantinian epoch, of the earthly with the divine city would, certainly, have caused the extinction of the latter on the earth, had it not set apart a distinct zone, of freedom and purification, which was the monastic life, so suddenly arising and rapidly developing throughout the newly-Christianised countries. None the less, in spite of the presence of such a spiritual counterbalance, the price paid, perhaps inevitably, for the 'conversion of Constantine' was the Rome of Alexander VI and Leo X. Sooner or later, bitter and almost mortal revolts are the outcome of conquests in which the victor is himself overcome.

The formation of the city of God cannot be reduced to, or merely superimposed upon, that of a city man aims at building on the denial, or at any rate the ignoring, of God. A society based on the profit-motive can never be, as such, a true beginning, and far less an implicit realisation, of the kingdom of God. Nor can one based on reaction against the profit-makers, on the part of those who want all to share in what hitherto had been appropriated by a few. In fact, any civilisation whose ruling principle is simply human control of material resources is neither Christian itself, nor capable, unchanged in its root, of becoming such. We are told that it is quite in order for man, while retaining control of the material world, to accept the governance of the spirit; but such a view overlooks what drives man to master the world, namely the desire for the satisfactions of sense at first, and then pride in his power, and this becoming ever more intense. At the root of our technological civilisation lies a moral attitude which cannot be changed at will. Man, by canalising all his energies for the satisfaction of material needs, creates fresh needs to which he becomes more and more enslaved. Once at the mercy of his voracious appetites, he is unable to accept moral obligations which appear to be so many restraints.

A world that has been humanised by, and on behalf of, mankind so constituted is no longer, as such, capable of serving a humanity that has regained consciousness of the scales against a conversion involving, for such a flouted in its resentment. All its weight is thrown into the scale against a conversion involving, for such a humanity, the rediscovery of these values and living by them. Mankind, in fact, can never be converted without first breaking with a world it has made to its own measure, but which now holds man imprisoned within this measure to which he has deliberately reduced himself.

Let us take an actual example, the discovery of nuclear fission, and the utilisation of atomic energy. Many who refrain from pursuing their reflections beyond the point where they would arouse misgivings, and, more especially, Christians who seem only too concerned to approve all that happens, without weighing objections, speak after this fashion: 'It is quite true that the first fruits of these discoveries were the destruction of Hiroshima and Nagasaki; but that was purely accidental. Man is under no necessity of continuing to turn these forces against himself. All he has to do is to make proper use of them, and they will ensure to all happiness, abundance and security. The curse of Genesis, "in the sweat of thy brow thou shalt eat bread", can now be wiped out in a single generation. The leisure all will be able to enjoy will open up marvellous possibilities for the human spirit.'

The scientists, on the other hand, even those who are not Christians, whose work has made the atomic bomb possible, are far from sharing this optimistic view, at least when they consider the persons who control, now and in the future, the fruits of their discoveries. Philip Oppenheimer, for example, is literally obsessed by the responsibility weighing on those who have placed such a frightful weapon at the disposal of men so obviously dominated by their desires of wealth and conquest. But what is even more disturbing is the way the very country which considers itself the chief upholder of human liberty and Christian civilisation has reacted to his scruples. It shows, in fact, that modern scientific discoveries do not take place in a mental climate of simple neutrality or indifference as regards their possible use. These discoveries and their application call for enormous expenditure, and those who provide the funds, whether states or individuals, obviously intend them to be used in furtherance of their own designs. If, then, the scientist finds that his conscience demands that his discoveries be applied in other ways than his masters desire, experience shows that he will simply be crushed. In a world where research in a particular field is geared to purposes of gain and dominion over others, the whole force of opinion, tacitly or openly, opposes the diversion of the resultant discoveries from the selfish and murderous aims for whose sake the necessary means had been provided.

Certainly, in the abstract, atomic energy is as well capable of beneficial, as of destructive, use; but, in the concrete, it is under the dominion of certain ends, which the human will insists on pursuing.

Here we come up against the world in the aspect in which it is characterised by St John. True, the world is, ultimately, the creation of God, and everything in it is basically good and capable of ministering to the good of man. Man, however, has organised it, as far as he can, not in accordance with the plan of God, but to serve his own ends, his selfish desires and pride of dominion. And, now that the world is organised in this way, it resists man, even when he wishes to change, and to change, in consequence, the order he has gradually set up. So it is that, when man sees the good and desires to bring it about, he finds himself caught between two opposing forces. One is within him, what St Paul calls 'the flesh', that second nature formed by the habit of sin, and which constitutes, at the very source, such an obstacle to the execution of our best intentions. Even if he managed to gain control of the 'flesh', man would still find himself opposed by the 'world'; and, the more it accords with the carnal side of man, the more it resists the spiritual. Furthermore, 'perfected' as it has been by carnal man, the world is now a kind of diabolical instrument to prevent man from becoming spiritual once more.

Suppose we grant that man refrains from the use of the atomic bomb through fear of the consequences, this fear also impels him to alter the present trend of industry so as to work solely for peaceful applications of nuclear energy. So long as the 'world' and the 'flesh' are what they are, such applications, directed to material satisfaction, will not bring the reign of charity one step nearer. They will only minister to fresh desires, stimulate new forms of pride, and, consequently, prepare the way for new enmities and oppressions; above all, far from setting the stage for the full reign of the Spirit in the world, they will only raise new obstacles to his appearance, and necessitate even more painful ruptures in man's habits of life.

We find ourselves, in fact, turning in a perpetual circle. To break away from the fatal course the world pursues, from the flesh as we know it to be, we need to make a breach in the world through which escape may be possible. The man who submits himself wholly to the views of the world, which are a kind of bog in which we entrap ourselves while pursuing the mirages of the flesh, such a man will never attain freedom. Always a prisoner of the world he can do nothing to save the world, but, cleaving blindly to it, will be carried along with it to his own perdition. To save the world, man must be liberated from it; but this he cannot be otherwise than by a general outlook which the world, the further it goes, makes it ever more difficult for him to adopt.

Some intervention there must be from above, taking us out of ourselves, while detaching us from the world. This does not mean that we must be taken away from the world, but we are to remain in it while no longer being of it, because we will have overcome the world. But what sort of a victory is it that is our own victory, and yet is beyond our scope? The victory that overcomes the world, says St John, is our faith.

The contemplation of the truths of faith, truths which did not enter the heart of man of themselves, does not unfit us for living in the world, nor does it involve necessarily that we flee the world. But, by freeing us from the world, it gives us, while still in the world, the sole means of saving it, while saving ourselves. No doubt, it will make our presence and our witness singularly unseasonable in the opinion of those whose only thought is to flatter the world; but unseasonable does not mean inappropriate. In times as tragic as the present, what seems most unseasonable may well be what is most urgent; for we have come to a point when, if the sleeper is not jolted back to consciousness, he is likely to die.

VII

SELF-DEVELOPMENT AND ASCETICISM

GOD loves man with an infinite love, yet we are told that 'it is a terrible thing to fall into the hands of the living God', for 'our God is a consuming fire'. God not only created man, but created him to his own image in so exact a sense that St Irenaeus could say: 'Gloria Dei vivens homo'—'man, in living, gives glory to God'. None the less, man cannot attain to life with God, except by undergoing the Cross. The Creator is also the Redeemer, and, as the epistle to the Hebrews says, there is no redemption without shedding of blood.

God, in creating us to his image, created us free, but, according to St Paul, we cannot be liberated by Christ without becoming, in the same measure, slaves of Christ and of God, even, too, of all mankind. It is in virtue of our intellect that we are most directly related to God, for by it we are destined to know him as he knows us. Yet it seems as if the natural procedure of the mind in its striving after universal knowledge is in constant conflict, or at any rate tension, with the certainties of the faith we receive from God. Though faith calls the mind into play, stimulates us to think and to reinvigorate our ideas, it still has to be accepted precisely as given; in one sense it is only too true that novelty in faith is synonymous with heresy.

The human mind, on the other hand, naturally

advances along constructive lines. Made, as he is, to the image of God, man has been placed in this world to bring its creation to fulfilment; but, in full career to the final conquest of matter, he comes up against a divine ordinance that seems to deny, not only the value, but the very scope, of his strivings, and to put forward a plan of God that would result, ultimately, in the complete breakdown of his own hopes. It would seem as if God, who affirms his surpassing love for man, turns out, in the end, to be his uncompromising enemy.

Is the Creator, then, who desires man to have life and to have it in abundant measure, contradicted by the Redeemer, who makes his appearance as a man of sorrows, and demands that all should take up their cross and follow him?

Is it possible that God, who made us free, should be jealous of our liberty, that, having given it us, he should think only of withdrawing it, or that he repented of his gift as soon as we began to use it?

It would almost seem as if God, who gave us a spiritual nature, is suspicious of the faculty of thought it involves, and, on every question, tries to impose on us judgments we would not have reached by ourselves; that, having made us capable of creation, he could not tolerate our works by the side of his own, or even within his own, and that he reserves to himself the right to intervene continually to destroy the work of our hands, and to substitute for it a heavenly city of his own building.

We have noticed each of these paradoxes in turn, but it will be observed that we have been careful not to claim to have set forth any simple solution. With regard to each, we have refused to deceive ourselves by choosing one or other alternative propounded. No less decisively do we reject the illusion that there is no real opposition, and that the two extremes are not so far apart as they appear. An example of undue simplification is the idea that it is one and the same thing that God should enjoin on us both life and death, since death to the body is life to the spirit. Such dialectical adroitness may well satisfy a Platonist, but is out of place in a religion of the Cross which is also a religion of the Resurrection.

The reader who has given some thought to the various themes we have pursued in turn will, by now, have concluded they all ultimately turn on the two apparently opposed poles of the creation and the redemption. How can the God of creation be also the God who imposes on us the cross? We must be quite clear that, if it is dishonest to pretend to solve the problem by suppressing one or other side of it, or to identify both by juggling with words, it would be still worse to develop, simultaneously, the consequences of the creation and those of the redemption, while rejecting any kind of co-ordination between them, or, indeed, any sort of interference. That would be, whether consciously or not, to lapse into some kind of dualism, which is the constant temptation of all gnostic systems. It cannot be denied that many modern systems that claim to be Christian are simply gross, though unavowed, forms of gnosticism. The only difference is that, while the early heretical gnostics exalted the God of the redemption over against the God of creation, our modern gnostics, by a singular inversion, always tend to exalt the Creator by contrast with the Redeemer.

A somewhat hasty critic, speaking of a book which tried to set out the real place, in the Christian life, of the mystery of Christ and the Cross, affirmed that, while all it said must be acknowledged as true, it was but half of the truth; that, if the Gospel contained nothing else, we would have to conclude that the Creator was no longer concerned with his creation, that he renounced being Creator; and that what we needed now, along with this theology of the Cross and the Resurrection, was a theology of the creation.

I admit that, with these words, he brings us right to the core of the problem facing modern man, the Christian in particular. At the same time, what he says seems to me an enormity in that it constitutes a clear admission that he has completely lost all idea of the meaning of the words he uses.

Let us go back to the central point of the objection. We are told that, if the Gospel consisted entirely in the mystery of the Cross and the Resurrection, we should have to conclude that the Creator had completely disinterested himself in his creation, that he had renounced, in fact, being Creator. This is such a monstrous conception in itself that we can scarcely bring ourselves to record it, and do so only because it shows clearly what lies at the root of a certain Faust-like Christianity, a kind of pseudo-theology of material realities, a so-called spirituality of the laity claiming to consecrate the secular sphere as it actually is, not to mention a host of other things paraded before us today which seem plausible enough until they manifest their fatuity by an enormity of this kind.

So then, the mystery of the Cross and the Resurrection, were it not completed or balanced in some way or other, would mean that the Creator had abandoned his creation, that he had renounced being Creator. But is it not perfectly plain that the whole of Christian tradition, the New Testament in its entirety, see, in Christ's Cross and Resurrection, the great proof that the Creator has not abandoned his creation? That God is our redeemer, far from implying that he has thereby relinquished the role of Creator, signifies that he ever continues it, notwithstanding all that has happened to sully his creation. Here we come to the crux of the whole matter, namely, that the redemption is not a kind of superfluity added to creation, a sublime piece of extravagance that might be tolerated if tucked into a corner but cannot be allowed to occupy the centre, still less the whole scene, where it would be shockingly out of place. To view it in this light would be to make the supernatural not something of a higher order than the natural, but something both alien to it and subverting it in its own sphere. Nothing could be more absurd. The redemption has meaning only as restoring and perfecting the creation, in line with God's original and immutable plan for it. The Cross, therefore, with its culmination in the Resurrection, is not just something for which a place must, of course, be found in human life, but which is not to be allowed to permeate it through and through, for fear of the work of creation being retarded; quite the contrary, it has become a necessity for the creation. Apart from the Cross, the creation is doomed to failure, and only by the Cross can it be saved, recovered, and brought to its true end.

The Creator and the Redeemer are not two different

gods in perpetual strife, to each of whom we must carefully distinguish his due, neither are creation and redemption two conflicting activities of a single God torn between two irreconcilable tendencies. In reality, creation and redemption are not, for God, distinct activities; they are one and the same action which pursues its course according to his original plan, despite all the obstacles it meets with. Redemption is simply creation attaining its end in spite of all; or better, it is creation triumphing over sin, which seemed to defeat it. The apparent opposition between God's creative and redemptive action arises solely from the changed conditions that the one divine action meets with once sin has happened.

That is why the first problem to which our reflections on God the Creator and Redeemer led us was the problem of liberty. It is the failure to take this question seriously enough, failure to see sin as the crux of the whole human problem, only to be solved by the Cross, that prevents so many Christians today from seeing how closely connected are creation and redemption.

All the seeming problems we have met with arise from the implicit assumption that God, when he became our Redeemer, brought into the world the Cross, which would never have come had he been content to be just Creator. No assumption could be more absurd than this, or more remote from reality.

It was not the redemption that brought the Cross, in other words, suffering and death, particularly of the innocent, into the world. The Redeemer did not bring them; they were already there, when he came.

Those who speak of the work of creation being somehow opposed to the work of redemption reveal, unconsciously, their servile acceptance of the principles of a false humanism whose fraudulent nature we have already exposed. They might as well say that, before the Gospel, there was no suffering in the world, and no one ever died; that man, following the bent of the creation, before the redemption interposed, was perfectly happy, unrestricted and untroubled; that he progressed freely in the discovery of a world in which all was harmony, in the outpouring of his creative activity, fulfilling himself in a world of perpetual spring.

Then, with the coming of Christianity, it seems that a gloom fell on all this. Suffering and death appeared for the first time. Man came to hate himself, and began to fear all that he was naturally inclined to. He lived in terror and grief, till the day came when modern humanism set him free, once and for all. He sighed with relief at being, once again, able to say, with the ancient poet: 'homo sum, humanum nihil a me alienum puto'.

All this is just a hopeless caricature of the facts, with every line distorted. What is now known as pre-Christian humanism never saw itself in the bright colours in which the neo-paganism of the Renaissance saw fit to deck it. When Terence uttered the words just quoted, what he meant was not: 'I am proud to be a man, and my delight is to savour all that life offers to man', but rather: 'I am no more than a man, and I am no stranger to any of his weaknesses'. Ancient humanity, in fact, was wholly obsessed with the problem of the sufferings of the innocent, the constant theme of Greek tragedy, and quite hallucinated by the ever-present and despairing vision of death; the Latin lyrics which are held to be a perfect expression of sane and joyful paganism are, really, a most pathetic expression of this feeling. The coming of Christianity, so far from casting a blight on a world hitherto serene and happy, brought, for the first time, the joy of liberation to a world which, the better it knew itself, the more aware it became of its enslavement.

Suffering and death, with all that baffles human understanding, were not brought into the world by Christianity; they were, we repeat, already there. It had only, in their regard, to point out the futility of the policy of opiates and palliatives, which hide evil from view for a moment, or else lull the mind into a reverie. It only dared to persuade man to look his destiny in the face without fear, because it placed in his hands the means to master it.

It is not merely that Christianity held out a more satisfactory explanation of suffering and death than those suggested by the religions and philosophies of antiquity. It provided something far greater, the ability to find in suffering and death the means to overcome them. Christianity alone was able to take over suffering and death in their most repugnant aspect, that is where the victim was wholly innocent, to make them serve the redemption of mankind. Hence it is that the redemption alone fulfils, restores and perfects creation, because it alone snatches the creation from destruction, turns the forces which would destroy it against themselves, and, by overcoming sin in death, prepares the ultimate defeat of death itself. When we say that the Cross is central in the whole Christian outlook, as the only possible salvation of all that is created, we do not mean that the Cross must occupy our whole vision of human life. The Cross of Christians, and of Christ, is, indeed, the suffering and death attendant on sinful man, but it is not only that. It would be an error vitiating our whole outlook to believe that suffering and death, by and in themselves, were the real good of man. They are nothing of the sort, according to the teaching of the Gospel, for to them is applicable the words of Christ, 'an enemy hath done this'. If the death of Christ is our salvation, that is because it kills death; in other words, because it is not just a death like all the others, but wholly exceptional. It is not death and suffering, as such, that save us, but it is what Christ, alone, has been able to make of his suffering and death.

Christ's Cross, and its replica that of the Christian, is, primarily, a suffering and death which are not just the inevitable consequence of sin, but the object of free and deliberate consent. Here again, we must be quite clear that this does not mean that the Cross is a kind of religious suicide, or that any form of suicide has anything in common with the Cross. The free and voluntary acceptance, essential to the Christian cross, consists in the acceptance of God's judgment on sin, which is also the supreme act of confident acceptance of his will, the act of a love abandoning itself wholly in response to the act of divine love giving itself without reserve.

What this means is that acceptance of the Cross begins with acknowledging the desperate state sin has brought us to, our total self-absorption, the self-seeking which has become an automatic reflex, the attitude of pride and covetousness adopted by man from the very beginning. Acceptance of the Cross, then, sees suffering and death, in the first place as a punishment intrinsic to sin which was their cause, as a disposition of the eternal justice which is inherent in the very nature of things, as God willed it to be, and which, of itself, makes manifest the essential malice of sin.

But, in addition, acceptance of the Cross sees in suffering and death, the outcome of sin, a disposition, not only of God's justice, but of his mercy. For the creature fated to die as a result of his attachment to self, his confinement to his own narrow aims, the ordeal of death can become the necessary means of detachment, of opening the way leading back from sin to faith in God, to the love which surrenders wholly to him who gave us all. First of all, however, this ordeal was, for the divine love itself, the means, paradoxical indeed and terrible, by which he showed the unalterable persistence of his generosity, a generosity exceeding any possible merit on the part of the creature. Consequently, man, in accepting the Cross, can never do more than respond to the initiative of the divine love by following the way it has already taken, along which he may allow it to draw him, but where he may never achieve equality with it, any more than he could have forestalled it.

None the less, the Cross can only achieve this when it is taken over into life as the result of a free decision involving the whole being, and after we have attained the full height of knowledge. In other words, for our cross to be one with that of Christ, it must come at the end, and, as it were, as the fulfilment, of an experience in which our whole nature is as completely developed as is possible in this life. This supposes, on the one hand, that our reflection on the world and our own life, illuminated by the Word of God and, in turn, explaining it, has brought us to understand, not only with the mind, but with the heart, indeed with our whole being, that all is love, all is a manifestation of the love of God, and, further, what is the nature of this love which has no parallel. This, in turn, supposes that we have grown into faith, that is, that this kind of knowledge can come only to one whose every potentiality implanted in him by the Creator has been gradually developed in harmony with these very discoveries of his. In this way, the discovery, and the perfecting of the mind which discovers, not only proceed on the same footing, but act on each other. We know the love of God, which is the basis of all real knowledge, only as we grow in this love, and we grow in it only by coming to know it more and more.

This need of being, as it were, conditioned for the Cross explains why Christ, while drawn to it as by a magnet from the first instant of his life on earth, yet repelled it, even went so far as to flee from it, so long as his 'hour' was not yet come. In the whole interval of time in which his human life was coming to maturity, he was growing, too, 'in wisdom and grace with God and men'. He experienced the world and man in the love of his immaculate mother, before discovering them anew in the frailties and blindness of his compatriots. He marvelled at the lilies of the fields before turning his face to Jerusalem and to death, the 'exodus' which awaited him there. He even passed for a man living at his ease by comparison with the austere life of John the Baptist. He shared in all natural human feelings, as we see in his spontaneous sympathy, not without a touch of irony, for the good Nathanael, a slight, if somewhat pretentious, theologian; his instinctive liking for the rich young man, notwithstanding the disappointment he was to occasion him; his friendship, though without illusions, for Peter; his tender affection for John; his boundless pity for the crowds pressing upon him; his especial sympathy for every kind of human sadness and joy. In all this, while giving ceaseless thanks to the Father for all things, he was making ready to leave the whole world, but only to regenerate and save it. As he said himself: 'I have received from the Father power to lay down my life, and power to take it up again'; and, the moment at last come, looking beyond the pains of his passion to the joy of the Resurrection, both for himself and all who belonged to him, he said: 'Father, the hour is come; glorify thy Son, that thy Son may glorify thee.'

This is what the life of the Christian should be, as, striving against sin by the power given him by the Spirit, he comes ever closer to identifying his life with that of Christ.

In our following of Christ, we awake to the presence in us of the old Adam, when we find, in the attraction of the world, both the attraction of God himself and the false lure of temptation. Our first victory over temptation is, emphatically, a first death to self, but it is, too, a first resurrection, a first discovery of the life of the new Adam. So it is that God, before the supreme moment when we have to consummate our life in total sacrifice, confronts us in various ways, through which we set about the process of leaving all things, and, at the same time, of making the discovery that nothing is accomplished except by sacrifice. Continually, with the advance of our creative activity, we are brought up against a choice of alternatives; either we allow all that we have gained to immobilise us and absorb us completely, or else to become a source of strength and light, on condition we really desire it, in our decision to make the gift of ourselves, that is, in one way or another, to relinquish all things.

In every stage of our life in the world and in the flesh, in each of which what comes from God and what is the result of sin are inseparably conjoined, we are called to renunciations that are, in fact, the only real fulfilments. In all that we come to acquire, we are, of necessity, faced with new temptations and summoned to fresh sacrifices, aided, though, by the light of the Gospel and the power of the grace which sets us free. When we yield to temptation, we think ourselves to be preserving what we have gained; but we are only hardening its crust or allowing it to seep away. When, however, we accept the sacrifice, we find again, on a higher plane, all that we renounced, and, on each occasion, discover, besides, things beyond our expectations. So it is that, in this life, all of us, Christian or not, work in the manner of ants who appear to be always starting again on something which is always coming to grief. Those, however, who reject faith in God, and are ignorant of his love, succeed only in slowly building up an ant-heap whose organisation, the more it grows, simply extends and perfects, with diabolical skill, the enslavement man has brought on himself. Others, by their faith, recognising and whole-heartedly accepting the presence of God both in their failures and successes, work for the building of the heavenly and eternal city both in the destruction of their earthly plans, which fails to make them despair, and in their finest successes, which cause them no illusion. It is a city already present in our midst, though as yet unseen, one which will, doubtless, be tried by fire, but will emerge from the fiercest ordeals purified from dross, and, in the end, adorned with a youthful beauty which is eternal.

The alternative, human or Christian, is a senseless one. To decide in favour of being man rather than Christian means, in the end, to be against man. To decide for Christianity, even if it is apparently against being human, means simply to decide for the death of the old man as a preliminary for the birth of the new. Ultimately, there is only the choice between being for oneself, which means, in fact, the world and the flesh being as they are, delivering oneself over to the devil, to sin and to death, or being for God, and, through the Cross, delivering oneself over to life, abundant life, the new life which is that of eternity.